BC to 1066

PER BELLVM PATRIA

Figure 1. An extract from the 13th century copy of the Roman linear map from India to Britannia – the *Tabula Peutingeriana* – of the part showing a curiously truncated south coast of Britannia: Richborough (Ratupis), Dover (Dubris), Canterbury (Duroaverus) and Lympne (Lemavio) are lower centre. North of the Thames parts of southern East Anglia are shown top left (north being to the left). North of that point the original which showed the rest of Britannia, and also the Iberian peninsula and western North Africa, has been lost. Bottom centre-left is Exeter (Iscadumno)

BC to 1066

An early history of eastern Sussex and the
Battle area from the Dawn of Time to
the Death of Edward the Confessor

Keith Foord

PER BELLUM PATRIA

Battle and District Historical Society Research Group 2020
Also published:
Neil Clephane-Cameron: *The Malfosse Walk,* 2nd edn, 2020
Keith Foord: *Conquest to Dissolution 1067–1538,* 2019
Keith Foord & Neil Clephane-Cameron: *1066 and the Battle of Hastings:
Preludes, Events and Postscripts,* 2015, 2016, 2018 (revised)
George Kiloh: *The Brave Remembered: Battle at War 1914–1919,* 2015
Adrian and Sarah Hall: *Edmund Langdon and his World,* 2018

ISBN: 978-1-903099-06-3

Copyright © Battle and District Historical Society 2020

First published in the UK in 2020
by the Battle and District Historical Society
c/o 16 Upper Lake, Battle, East Sussex TN33 0AN
Tel: 01424 775590 / 07836 522257
E-mail: neil@clephane-cameron.com
Contact: Neil Clephane-Cameron, Honorary Secretary
www.battlehistory,btck.co.uk

Typeset in Garamond by Helm Information
amandahelm@uwclub.net

The cover image is derived from the 'Franks Casket', dated about 700CE, now in the
British Museum. For more details, see p. 139.
The image has been magnified, image smoothed and recoloured, and is derived
from a photograph by John W. Schulze in Wikimedia Commons.
Creative Commons Attribution 2.0 Generic licence.

Printed and bound in Great Britain by
CPI Group (UK) Ltd, Croydon CR0 4YY

Contents

List of Figures

List of Tables

Abbreviations commonly used in the text

ASC Anglo-Saxon Chronicle
BCE Before the Common Era
BT Bayeux Tapestry
CE Common Era
DB Domesday Book
L Latin
OE Old English
OF Old French
OFr Old Frisian
ON Old Norse
SAC Sussex Archaeological Collections
TRE In the time of King Edward (i.e. before the Conquest)

Figure 2. A complete gold Stater of King Verica of the Atrebates dating to the period 10–35 CE

Figure 3.
Top: A gold Roman solidus of Constantius II, about 350–355 CE

Bottom: An incomplete early medieval silver penny of Offa of Mercia (757–96 CE).

Foreword

There are two main reasons why what is usually called Local History needs to be written. The first is to record facts about places and people which would otherwise be unknown. The second is to bring alive the people and the communities that are the bedrock of all societies, be they regional, national, or international. Keith Foord's book is a huge success on both counts. A reader will be able to make his or her way from the historical geology of eastern Sussex and the Battle area in pre-historic times to the year 1066 when the region was the setting for a battle that transformed English, British and European history. Every reader will find sections which they find especially interesting and inspiring. For myself, having never lived anywhere near eastern Sussex, but having often visited, it is the sheer dynamism of the region's history that Keith Foord brings alive. He is constantly aware of the need to place its history in a national context and also in a cross-Channel setting as well as to focus on the local. France and the Low Countries are never far away. At the same time places and people are brought to life. There were many times when I found myself wanting to visit the churches and villages about which he writes so scrupulously and vividly. And, given my personal historical interests, I was fascinated by the detailed reconstruction of the region's society in the decades before the year 1066 and the events that changed so much in eastern Sussex and elsewhere.

Professor David Bates
President, Battle and District Historical Society,
2020

'We open our mouths and out flow words whose ancestries we do not even know… In a single sentence of idle chatter we preserve Latin, Anglo-Saxon, Norse: we carry a museum inside our heads, each day we commemorate peoples of whom we have never heard.'

Penelope Lively

A Timeline of Events influencing Eastern Sussex until 1066

4.5B ago	Earth formed.
165–145M ago	Upper Jurassic period, Purbeck limestone beds including Sussex Marble formed. Seams of gypsum can be found in these beds.
145M–125M ago	Wealden sedimentary rocks (sandstones, shales and clays) formed by erosion of igneous, metamorphic and pre-existing sedimentary rocks.
125–100M ago	Lower greensand, followed by gault clay/upper greensand strata formed
100–66M ago	Chalk and flint strata formed.
70–75M ago	Uplift of the Wealden anticline.
0.5 to 1M ago	Chalk anticline ridge between Britain and France is breached multiple times. Megafloods form English Channel.
230,000BCE	Homo Neanderthalensis spread northwards.
Before 150,000BCE	Homo Sapiens evolves in Africa.
27,000BCE	Peak of Last Glacial maximum.
20,000BCE	Last glacial maximum ends.
12,000BCE	Last glacial maximum ends.
10,900–9,600BCE	Loch Lomond (Younger Dryas) stadial. 900 years long drop in temperature, humans retreat south.
9500–2500BCE	Development of woodland in the Weald.
8000–3000BCE	Substantial rise in sea levels. Eastern Sussex embayments form. Doggerland the last low-lying land-bridge between eastern England and continental Europe floods.
7800–4000BCE	Late Mesolithic activity in Combe Haven valley.
4000–25BCE	Neolithic activity in Combe Haven valley.
2500–800BCE	Bronze Age activity in Combe Haven valley.
1400–1100BCE	Mountfield Bronze Age gold hoard buried.
1400–600BCE	Rapid social development and population growth.
800–600BCE	Start of Iron Age
500–300BCE	Start of movement of Belgae into south-east Britain from north-west Gaul.
75BCE	Atrebate Belgae move into southern Britain.
55 & 54BCE	Julius Caesar's first Roman expeditions to Britain.

From 50BCE	Iron working at Upper Wilting.
31BCE	Roman coins for this date and before found at Ashburnham.
43CE	Romans invade and occupy.
About 197	Reforms of Severus. Britannia split into two Provinces, with Britannia Prima to the south.
249	Last historical record of the Classis Britannicus.
250	Major Roman iron working ends in eastern Sussex.
284–305	Diocletian reforms the Roman empire, with separation of military and civilian functions.
286	Count of the Saxon Shore appointed.
287	Carausius usurps Britannia and northern Gaul.
293	Anderita (Pevensey) Roman castle started, possibly by Carausius. Carausius assassinated by Allectus.
296	Britannia recovered by Constantius I. Britannia becomes a 'diocese' of four provinces, south-eastern province called 'Maxima Caesariensis'.
306	Constantine the Great proclaimed Emperor. Diocletian reforms completed.
313	Edict of Milan – Christianity tolerated in Roman Empire.
350	Magnentius proclaimed Caesar in Gaul and seizes Britannia.
353	Defeat of Magnentius, Constantine II recovers Gaul and Britannia.
367	Britannia beset by a period of turmoil termed the 'Barbarica conspiratio'. Comes maritime tractus and possibly also the Dux Britannicus killed.
368	Flavius Theodosius recovers Britannia and Hadrian's Wall repaired.
382	Magnus Maximus is proclaimed Emperor in Britannia.
388	Magnus Maximus defeated and Valentinianus II becomes Emperor of the Western Roman Empire.
398	Roman victories over invading Picts, Scotti and 'Saxones', but troops start to be withdrawn from Britannia.
406	Marcus proclaimed in Britannia, but there is a major incursion of Germanic tribes into Gaul.
407	Constantine III proclaimed in Britannia. Many Roman troops removed from Britannia to northern Gaul to fight the barbarians.
409	Britannia revolts and Roman rule effectively ends in Britannia.
About 425–470	Sociological and economic collapse, followed by slow recovery, more marked in south.
446	Romano-Britons appeal for help to Aetius to no avail.
447–449	First 'Germanic' settlement in Kent. Bede records 'arrival of the English'.

455	Battle of Aylsford (Kent) between Romano-British and Hengist and Horsa. Horsa killed and replaced by Hengist's son Oisc.
456	Battle of Crayford. Romano-British retreat to London.
465	Battle of Wipped's Creek (possibly in west Surrey/north Hampshire area).
About 470	A Romano-British Celtic army is said to have defeated a Saxon army. This event has been conflated to encompass Arthurian mythology.
473	Romano-British leaders flee to north and west.
477	Ælle (Saxon) lands in western Sussex, probably near Selsey.
485	Battle of Mearcredsburn (possibly at Penhurst, near present day Battle).
488	Oisc becomes King of Kent. Founds Oiscingas dynasty.
491	South Saxons wipe out Romano-Britons at Pevensey.
568	Wessex expanding aggressively.
597	Sent by the Pope, Saint Augustine arrives in Kent.
600	Possible first use of term Hæstingas to describe eastern Sussex.
603	First meeting between Saint Augustine and Celtic Church leaders, latter unimpressed.
607	West Saxons under Ceolwulf attack South Saxons.
661	Sub-king Aethelwalh of Sussex (under Wulfhere of Mercia).
675	Jutish Meonwara (S. Hampshire) and Wihtwara (Isle of Wight) added to Sussex by Wulfhere.
681	Selsey Abbey founded by Saint Wilfrid of Northumbria.
685	Eadric of Kent may have ceded Hæstingas to the South Saxons.
686	Caedwalla of Wessex takes control of Surrey, Sussex and Kent.
688–695	Laws of King Ine of Wessex.
692	Sub-king Nunna of Sussex.
694	Wihtred of Kent and Ine of Wessex agree borders of Sussex.
700	About now the neighbouring area of Kent is called Limenwara (people of Limen). Beginning of the development of 'dens' in the Weald.
764	Offa of Mercia turns on Kent.
770	Offa subjugates Sussex, except Hæstingas. First recorded use of name Hæstingas.
771	Offa defeats the Hæstingas.
772	Offa grants lands to support a minster church at Bexhill.
790	Offa grants lands at Pevensey, Hastings and Rotherfield to the Abbey of Saint Denis in Paris.
800	Old Winchelsea may have been established about now.

825	Wessex takes control of Sussex which becomes a province of Wessex.
843	Large Viking raid near Romney.
870	Vikings attack all south coast.
871	Alfred routs Vikings at the battle of Ashdown, becomes King of Wessex.
878	Danes defeated at Battle of Edington, Treaty of Wedmore.
886	Partition treaty creates the Danelaw, Sussex remains under English laws.
890	Burghal forts at Hæstingaceastre and Eorpeburnan (possibly Newenden).
892	Danish fleet lands at Appledore, Kent. Probably attack Eorpeburnan burghal fort which was incomplete..
899	King Alfred dies.
900	Alfred's will gives Beckley and Rotherfield royal estates to his blood kinsman Osferth.
928	Mint recorded at Hæstingaceastre.
980	Viking raids resume.
982	Eadwine, Ealdorman of Sussex dies. Rameslie manor (Rye to Hastings area) bequeathed to Æthelmaer, the founder of Eynsham Abbey, by his kinswoman Wulfwyn, Abbess of Wareham.
983	Start of reign of King Sweyn Forkbeard in Denmark.
993	Hæstinga lege (Hastingsleigh) recorded.
994	Massive Viking raids along south coast.
999	Viking raids into Kent probably affected Hæstingas.
1002	King Æthelred II marries Princess Emma of Normandy. May promise to give Rameslie to the Abbey of Fécamp in Normandy.
1005	King Æthelred II confirms Eynsham Abbey, founded by Æthelmaer - its endowments still include Rameslie.
1009	Large Viking army lands in Kent, paid off with Danegeld and ravage Sussex instead.
1011	Vikings overrun all Kent, Surrey, Sussex and Hæstingas.
1013	Æthelmaer dies, but Æthelred fails to pass Rameslie to the Abbey of Fécamp. King Sweyn of Denmark invades England via Lincolnshire, becomes king by conquest but dies 5 weeks later.
1014	Æthelred returns.
1015	Cnut, son of Sweyn invades, via Poole harbour and River Frome. Strikes north into Wiltshire. By the winter Wessex submits.
1016	Fighting between Edmund Ironside (son of Æthelred II by his first wife) and Cnut. Æthelred dies. Ironside and Cnut share rule of England. Ironside dies and Cnut is king of all England.

1017	Executions of high-ranking Englishmen. Godwin Wulfnothson survives. Cnut marries Æthelred's widow, Emma. Cnut gives Rameslie to Fécamp Abbey.
1018	Godwin appointed Earl of eastern Wessex, excluding Kent.
1020	Godwin appointed Earl of all Wessex, still excluding Kent. Godwin marries Cnut's brother in law's sister, Gytha Thorkelsdóttir, a Danish noblewoman.
1022	Harold Godwinson born.
1027/1029	William of Normandy born, father Duke Robert of Normandy.
1028	Second charters give manor of Brede to Fécamp abbey, adjacent to the lands of Rameslie.
1030	Possible marriage of Cnut's widowed sister Margaret-Estrith to Robert of Normandy – rapidly rejected or annulled.
1035	King Cnut dies. Harold I (Harefoot), son of Æthelred II and his first wife holds England, after excluding his half-brother Harthacnut who was holding Wessex. Harthacnut remains King of Denmark. Duke Robert dies on pilgrimage. William becomes Duke William II of Normandy.
1036	Alfred, younger son of Æthelred II and Emma and brother of Edward murdered. Earl Godwin involved.
1040	Harefoot dies. Harthacnut, son of Cnut and Emma becomes King of England and cedes Denmark
1041	Edward, son of Æthelred and Emma, who has lived a life of exile in Normandy is invited to join his mother Emma, and his half-brother Harthacnut in England as co-ruler/heir presumptive.
1042	Harthacnut dies.
1043	Edward crowned king.
1044	Harold Godwinson made Earl of East Anglia.
1047	Battle of Val ès Dunes, victory for King Henri I of France and William, Duke of Normandy against Guy of Burgundy, who was related to William.
1048	Viking raids on Kent, chased off by English navy recruited from the future Cinque Ports.
1049	Edward arranges blockade of the Channel to assist Emperor Henry III against Baldwin V of Flanders.
1051	Near civil war between Edward and the Godwins. The Godwins were banished. William of Normandy may have visited Edward and been promised the throne of England if Edward had no sons or other direct heirs.
1052	Godwins restored but gives hostages to Edward. Edward's hostages – the youngest son of Godwin, Wulfnoth and his grandson Hàkon Sweynson are taken to Normandy and the 'care' of Duke William.

1053	Earl Godwin Wulfnothson dies. Harold Godwinson becomes Earl of Wessex.
1054	Battle of Mortemer, victory for William of Normandy. Imprisons Guy of Ponthieu.
1054/55	The cartulary of Fécamp records the gift from King Edward of saltpans at Pevensey and a church at Borne ((Eastbourne).
1056	Harold meets with Baldwin V of Flanders and the released Guy of Ponthieu at St Omer. Emperor Henry III dies.
1057	Battle of Dives, another victory for William. Edward, son of Edmund Ironside returns to England with his family but dies. His son Edgar Atheling is brought up at Edward the Confessor's court.
1062–63	Probable oath to support Edgar Atheling as heir to Edward.
1064	Harold sets sail from Bosham. The objective of this voyage is unknown, but Harold Godwinson lands in Ponthieu, was held by Guy of Ponthieu, then taken to Normandy and 'entertained' by William of Normandy. He returns with his hostaged nephew Hàkon but not his youngest brother Wulfnoth. William believes that Harold has become his 'liege' man and has sworn on holy relics to support his claim to the English throne.
1065	Tostig Godwinson deposed as Earl of Northumbria. Goes to Flanders and starts to plot vengeance and find allies.
1066	Edward dies. Harold crowned King of England. William furious and plans invasion of England. Norwegian Harold Hardrada and Tostig Godwinson invade England via the Humber estuary. Earls Morcar of Northumbria and Edwin of Mercia lose Battle of Fulford, near York, against Hardrada and Tostig. Harold wins Battle of Stamford Bridge against the invaders led by Harald Hardrada and his estranged brother Tostig, who were both killed. Harold then loses the Battle of Hastings, where he and his brothers Garth and Leofwine and many other leading English thanes are killed. William crowned King of England at Christmas.

Introduction

'One God, one law, one element,
And one far-off divine event,
To which the whole creation moves.'
Alfred the Great

How had the previous people – tribes, invaders and rulers – of eastern Sussex arrived, settled and lived before the Normans came in 1066? How did the land and coastline of eastern Sussex that formed the background of their lives evolve, and what did the settlements look like, what were they called and where were they?

Eastern Sussex as we see it today must have been nearly coterminous with an ancient sub-region named after the men and women called Hæstingas – the people of Hæsting – which may have been so called from the 6th to the early 11th centuries. The area appears to have been sociologically and culturally influenced somewhat more by the Kingdom of Kent to the east than the rather fragmented sub-kingdoms of Sussex to the west.

Most of the district shares its inland topography with the High Weald, but there are low-lying coastal areas of former estuaries and marshlands between Pevensey and Bexhill, and at Combe Haven and east of the Fairlight cliffs.

Coastal townships, the forebears of Rye, Old Winchelsea, Hastings, Bexhill and Pevensey, evolved from small coastal hamlets. Inland villages and hamlets developed near pockets of good agricultural land with access to water or at the junctions of tracks. The site of the present town of Battle, which did not exist then, was a hilly scrubby place at the junction of ancient tracks. Here a low ridge extends towards Bexhill and a higher ridge of sandstone starts to stretch from the High Weald towards the sea at Hastings, east of which it ends in some rather spectacular cliffs – around Hastings, Fairlight, Bexhill and Pett are the only places where these Wealden sandstone and clay formations still meet the sea.

On each side of the Battle ridge are watersheds. On the western side the streams run towards the small Combe Haven or Asten river which enters the sea at Bulverhythe, between St Leonards-on-Sea and Bexhill, where there was once a small harbour. Slightly further north-westwards the Ashburn stream feeds through Ashburnham to the Wallers

Haven river which flows across what was a large shallow Pevensey embayment, now drained marshland. To the east the flow is via tributaries to the River Brede and thence to the once also embayed waters of the 'Rye Camber' or 'Camera Romaneo' – now the Pett Level marshes, Rye Harbour and Dungeness. Further to the north-east watersheds from the High Weald feed the rivers Rother (formerly the Limen) and Tillingham which also fed into the Camera Romaneo.

At the northern end of what was essentially a Hastings peninsula a narrow neck of high land connects the Battle ridge to the High Weald. This neck was where the English and Norman armies would clash in 1066 and define the future of England and much of the English-speaking world.

Although partially cut off by the stretches of marsh and water on each side and the vast Andreadsweald forest to the north, eastern Sussex has been inhabited and used by man from at least the Neolithic age. It was well known to the Romans, even ahead of their invasion, as a source of iron ore – and importantly abundant wood from which to create the charcoal to smelt it to make iron.

As time went by small fishing ports developed. These later became important for a while, as part of the Cinque Ports confederation, in defending the developing English nation, providing ships and sailors for English earls and the royal fleets. Then the earliest ports lost protecting cliffs and shingle banks to wild storms and sea erosion. Its small harbours were destroyed or diminished, gradually silting up one by one and fading.

Fortunately, we have some early detail from Rye and Old Winchelsea, mainly related to the large manor of Rameslie, within which they both lay. Also, some information about Bexhill and Pevensey, but less detail from the villages. Sadly, there is not as much as we might wish from Hastings' very early days, although much can be inferred.

This book brings together what can be found of direct relevance to eastern Sussex before 1066, from the time of formation of the lands and coastline to the start of the year of that decisive battle. It is an admittedly somewhat unbalanced book as the amount of information available waxes and wanes through the centuries, from before humans existed to its earliest settlers, through the times when Romans, Saxons (or more likely Jutes and Frisians), Danes and kings came and went. Sometimes a small item is grasped at as an illustration; sometimes it is something more momentous or just prosaic. The chapters are in general time order from the dawn of creation to 1066.

Most interpretations seen here are echoes of some sometimes quite intense academic studies, involving early oral and written histories, geology, historical geography, place-name studies, genetics and archaeology. A wide range of sources has been used including extracts from various PhD theses and esoteric summary papers, sometimes found in unexpected places after chasing up a tiny phrase or clue from elsewhere. A sort of second sense slowly evolved about what to find where, and when to apply some degree of circumspection if some frankly cranky ideas emerged, particularly from the internet, but also from the loquacious and sometimes over imaginative and zealous writers of the 18th and 19th centuries. What are avoided are some of the more didactic early interpretations, particularly from the Victorian era which, whilst certainly vigorous, had little regard for the past or sensitivities. They often adopted a straight-line and nationalistic approach to the period covered by this book. These did not allow for the more analytic, flexible and lateral analyses demanded to interpret the time before 1066, which is so full of uncertainties, grey areas and sometimes very black holes. This leads in a few areas to the author's subsequent wonderings about alternative conclusions.

The book starts with a précis of the main points of historical geology and geography of eastern Sussex, which are essential to an understanding of why the area evolved as it did. It then moves on to report on the most recent genetic studies of how south-east England was populated after the end of the last glacial maximum in about 20,000BCE. Please note that these two chapters are very much lay overviews of complicated subjects. They are here to set the scene for the later contexts and are only broad interpretive reports.

The general history follows, with a look at eastern Sussex in pre-historic and Roman times. It then moves forward through the development of the 'kingdom' of Sussex, particularly in its relationships with Kent and Wessex, and hunts for information around and about the slightly enigmatic people and district called Hæstingas. Finally, in the post-Alfredian period, after 900, we move into the years of English and Danish rule, critical to what happened in 1066 and try to determine what eastern Sussex was like at that crucial time.

This is a period when much has depended on archaeology and its interpretation because the written history is so 'thin'. Historical arguments have been fierce and there are many uncertain areas and many gaping chasms in our knowledge. The author can only say that he has done his best to sort fact from fiction and fantasy and to describe the history in a coherent way. Some readers will undoubtedly query some interpretations and conclusions. All the author can ask is that whenever possible questioners try to go back to the best modern sources that they can find and analyse for themselves what they discover. History is always moving on and even interpretations from even ten to thirty years ago are sometimes challenged. New sources continue to be uncovered, sometimes found in the most unlikely places, what the French call 'au derrière les fagots' (in a dusty old corner behind the firewood), and novel scientific techniques are being applied to historical population studies and archaeological findings.

This is a history focussed on eastern Sussex, uniquely influenced by the Weald, marshlands and the sea. This is not a history of all Sussex, for the history of Sussex west of Eastbourne is somewhat different given that the South Downs and the western coastal plain have presented a dissimilar and to a degree richer historical picture and received little or no influence from Kent. Nor is it a history of England, although events elsewhere are touched on when necessary, for this book focusses on the south-east and its own migratory history

The author must thank Dr David Alderton for geological advice, Professor David Bates (for a huge amount of useful information, critiques, encouragement and advice), both Lynn Cornwell and Kevin Cornwell for archaeological advice, Neil Clephane-Cameron for proof reading and original ideas particularly about William and Harold's interactions, George Kiloh and Dr Patrick Malone for proof reading, technical advice, and critical comments, Dr Peter Greene for photographic support, Amanda Helm for setting the proofs of the book to her exceptional standards, and fellow members of BDHS Research Group Adrian and Sarah Hall and Gina Doherty for their suggestions and general support and all other BDHS Committee members for agreeing to publish this book. And as always, his wife, for a lot of patience and all those cups of tea and coffee.

Of course, any errors, actual or interpretive and spelling mistakes are the author's, although much is spelt 'as found' and this can give rise to interesting variations. Any inadvertent breach of copyright is apologised for and will be corrected in any future printing.

'The creation of the world did not occur at the beginning of time, it occurs every day.'

Marcel Proust, 1925

'How helpless any one is who, without a competent knowledge of the dynamics of geology, attempts to read the riddles of the past.'

Augustus Jessopp, 1894

Figure 4. Located in the northern hemisphere constellation of Ursa Major (the Great Bear), the nearby galaxy Messier 81 (also known as also known as Bode's Galaxy) is easily visible through binoculars or a small telescope.
NASA/JPL-Caltech

Discovered by the German astronomer Johann Elert Bode in 1774, this is one of the brightest galaxies in the night sky. Messier 81 is located at a distance of 12 million light-years from Earth and reminds us of our place in the universe.

1

Asteroids, Dinosaurs, Ice Ages, Plate Tectonics, Rocks, Sea-levels and Volcanos: Eastern Sussex over the Eons

The Earth is reckoned to be more than 4.5 billion years old. Such an age is as difficult to imagine as the size of the cosmos and the realisation that Earth is a tiny planet orbiting an average-sized star called the Sun, towards the edge of our galaxy – the Milky Way – which is itself one of an unending array of galaxies.

As the primordial earth cooled and vast seas were created there followed extended periodic cycles of cooling and re-warming. The reasons for this are very complicated and involve astronomical cycles affecting the Earth's orbit and its varying distance from its heat source (the Sun), regular and irregular variations in solar surface activity, the composition of the atmosphere, particularly of the amounts of greenhouse gases, such as carbon dioxide and methane, volcanic eruptions, asteroid impacts, plate tectonics and ocean flows. Earth has aged and over the eons it has evolved, and its surface geology that we see today was formed.

Surface Rocks of eastern Sussex

The surface rocks and soils of most of eastern Sussex today are in the sedimentary group, derived from sediments from the erosion of the primordial igneous, metamorphic and pre-existing older sedimentary rocks over billions of years. These sediments first formed the Lower Cretaceous Wealden sandstone, shales and clays 145–125 million years ago and then the lower greensand and gault clay/upper greensand after 125 million years ago. The iron siderite (carbonate) deposits within the sandstones, to be so important in the later industrial history of eastern Sussex, formed in layers within the sandstones and shales under anoxic and highly alkaline conditions related to mats of decaying microorganisms.

Then the gault clay stratum of southern England started to be overlaid by chalk. Chalk formed during the warm Upper Cretaceous Period ('only' 100–66 million years ago) when the clays and sandstones were covered at a time of global high sea levels with warm salt oceans. Myriads of tiny sea creatures lived in those oceans, and when they died their skeletons and shells fell to the sea floor and formed deposits of chalk (mainly as calcium carbonate). Silica also dissolved out from the skeletons of these creatures and, under some very specific localised bacterial and acidic conditions on the seabed, formed silica nodules called flints, which became embedded in layers in the chalk. These flints were later to be used by early man for flint tools and as a very hard building material. Chalk is too soft to build with, although useful cements can be made from it.

On occasion, before the Cretaceous periods and during the pre-Wealden Upper Jurassic Period some gypsum (calcium sulphate dihydrate) crystallised out from pockets of saturated brine and some of this was laid down in the Brightling and Mountfield areas north of Battle. It is associated with the Purbeck Beds in our area, which contain both blue and grey limestone and within which can be found a rare hard form of limestone formed in freshwater lakes, called Sussex marble, similar to, but coarser than, Purbeck marble (figure 5). The pillars of the font at St Mary's Church in Battle are made from this (figure 6) and some was used in the cloister of the demolished church of Battle Abbey. Local 'blue' limestone has been used for polished paving slabs at Penhurst church, and for memorial slabs in local churchyards, e.g. at Brightling. Some grey and blue limestone rubble was used in the building of Mountfield Church.

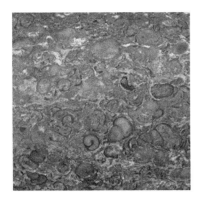

Figure 5. Sussex 'marble' formed from the shells of freshwater gastropods and winkles. Sometimes called 'Winklestone' for very obvious reasons. Public Domain

Figure 6. The font at St Mary's Church, Battle. Font image © Peter T Greene

The Sussex landscape today shows the features of all these layers which were 'folded up' in the middle to form what is called an anticline by enormous compressive forces as the earth's tectonic plates moved, about 30 million years ago. The strata were pushed up and the highest point in the area possibly achieved a height of nearly 1,000 metres (3,300 feet), just short of the height of Snowdon. Over further eons these were eroded by water and ice, with the overlying soft chalk being completely eroded away over the dome of the High Weald, whose maximal height is now 225 metres (740 feet) at Crowborough Beacon (Figure 7).

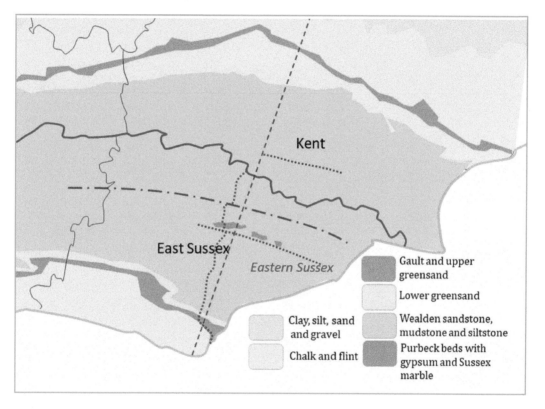

Figure 7 (a and b, both illustrative only) The Wealden Anticline across eastern Sussex

Above: Figure 7a shows the dominance of the surface Wealden sandstones. The brown dash-dot line shows the apex of the anticline and the brown dotted lines major geological faults.

Overleaf: Figure 7b is the section north-south of the dashed purple line in 7a, demonstrating the erosion of upper strata after the anticline uplift

Derived from information in Aldiss et al and multiple online sources. The vertical dimension in 7b is exaggerated for illustrative effect. Both images © Keith Foord

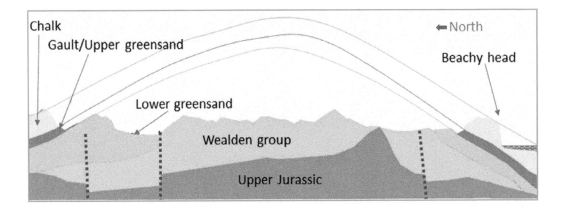

The flint nodules released from the chalk strata were moved to make the huge shingle beds of the English Channel. The harder sandstones formed the hills of the Weald that we see today. A very crude estimate of the total volume of rock removed by the processes gives an amount of nearly 5 trillion cubic metres or 12.5 trillion tonnes of rock removed from over eastern Sussex alone, unimaginable quantities (for the curious this calculation is based on an oblate dome with a height of 750m and diameter 35km).

The hardest sandstones formed the hills and ridges of the Weald and some of the eroded sand and clay silts deposited in the valleys. Along the Battle to Heathfield ridge there are small outcrops of older Upper Jurassic Purbeck beds, elsewhere these are deep to the Wealden sandstones.

The enormous quantities of eroded rock, sand, silt and flints ended up moved by ice or washed downstream. During an Ice Age the deposits would have been pushed by glaciers moving from the north into the area of the English Channel, with the chalk eventually being re-dissolved into the seas and the sands, silts and flints deposited in huge moraines.

These moraines in turn would become the gravel and shingle banks of the English Channel. In later times still, as the sea levels rose above these beds as the glaciers melted and retreated, these huge deposits of shingle and sand would be able to be shifted by tides and storms and markedly affect the eastern Sussex coastline – which is ever changing.

The remaining features of the chalk which can be seen from eastern Sussex are the South Downs which extend westwards from Eastbourne. Fine views of the chalk cliffs of Beachy Head can be seen on the western horizon over Pevensey Bay from the Battle ridge.

Between Hastings and Cliff End, which is where the highest part of the Wealden ridge meets the sea, there are some spectacular mudstone and sandstone sea-cliffs where the layering described above can be clearly seen (Figure 8). Along the coast

Figure 8. The sandstone cliffs at Hastings   Photo: © Keith Foord

between Cooden and Pett dinosaur footprints dating from 100 to 145 million years ago have been found from time to time, over many years, the first discovery being about 160 years ago. These are normally found after cliff erosion uncovers an interface between mudstone and overlying sandstone layers. Most recently (between 2014 and 2018) a large number of high-quality footprints from multiple species of dinosaur were identified by University of Cambridge researchers following cliff erosion near Fairlight. This work has been reported by Shillito and Davies.

Looking eastwards from the Battle Ridge and from Fairlight into Kent the North Downs can also be seen, mirroring the South Downs on the other side of the anticline.

Ice Ages

It is estimated that there have been at least five and maybe up to nine major Ice Ages that have affected the geology and biology of Earth. The last was called the Late Cenozoic Ice Age which began 34 million years ago. This was a relatively warm period, but during the last two million years temperatures regularly were freezing with an alternating pattern of glacial and interglacial periods – this pattern remains ongoing at present. This definitely affected the small numbers of Neanderthals, possibly the first humans to live in England, who drifted into southern Britain after about 230,000BCE as they had to retreat by 180,000BCE as cold fluctuations recurred.

The Last Glacial Maximum (LGM), also known as the Weichselian glaciation, that affected the British Isles was an advance of a very cold zone southwards. This began only 33,000 years ago, which amounts in time to a mere blink of a geological eye.

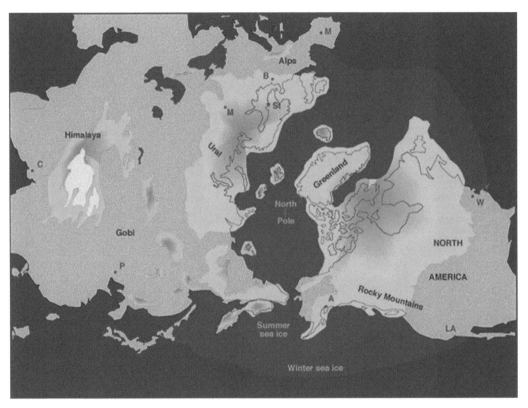

Figure 9. The Last Glacial Maximum. Note this is a north polar view, the UK and Ireland are located upside down just below and right of top centre
Hannes Grobe/AWI / CC BY (https://creativecommons.org/licenses/by/2.5) redrawn, supplemented and modified graphic from John S. Schlee 'Our changing continent', United States Geological Survey (2000)

Figure 9 shows a North Polar view of the extent of this glaciation. This involved the British Isles maximally 27,000 years ago. It will be noted that the southern coast of England was (just) not glaciated. But it would have been very far from comfortable as it would have been in a zone of arctic desert/tundra. The seas around the UK to the west, south and north were frozen over in winter. What is not clear from this diagram is the thickness of this Northern Hemisphere glaciation, which had 3 to 4 km (2 to

2½ miles) thick ice sheets. The water tied up in that huge amount of polar ice caused a global sea-level fall of about 125 metres (400 feet).

This LGM before our era extended across northern France, southwards as far as Hungary and clearly involved all Scandinavia and the Baltic countries. It peaked in about 27,000BCE and ended about 20,000BCE. This is when there was a very extensive land-bridge between Britain and continental Europe, but any humans attempting to live in the area of southern England would have still had a very hard time indeed to survive in the bitter cold. To the west, south and north the sea would freeze in winter, almost to Spain. After this LGM the ice retreated northwards and the dry land-bridge connecting the British Isles to the European mainland gradually disappeared below the sea over the next 20,000 years. There was one last cold sting in the tale after the LGM. In about 10900BCE there was a nine-hundred-years-long cold spell, called the Loch Lomond or Younger Dryas stadial when temperatures dropped 15°C. This briefly pushed humans back south again, but once it was over they returned, and this group became our forebears.

But what about the land-bridge to mainland Europe? The last vestige of it was the low lying Doggerland across the southern North Sea area, which was inundated by the rising sea about 8,500 years ago (figure 10). It is chastening to recognise that we still exist during an interglacial retreat northward.

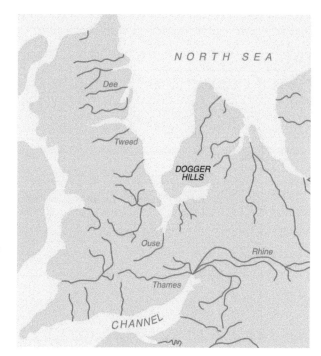

Figure 10. The land bridge: map of Northern Europe at the time of Doggerland
© By Max Naylor - Own work, CC BY-SA 3.0, https://commons.wikimedia.org/w/index.php?curid=6011686

The English Channel and the coastlines

Long before the LGM, one million to half a million years earlier there was a chalk 'dam' across what is now the Strait of Dover. The remains of the ends of this can be seen at Dover and across the Channel around Cap Gris Nez, and it is not difficult to imagine the missing low chalk ridge between the two. This ridge would have acted as a huge dam to trap water between it and the retreating North Sea glacier in a huge lake covering the southern North Sea. This reservoir contained all the melt water from the glacier and water from all the rivers draining into the Baltic and North Seas from the south, including large rivers such as the Rhine, Elbe, Oder and Vistula (figure 11). Some water must have drained via a river down the central English Channel via a narrow isthmus through a low chalk ridge, but eventually this gap was just not big enough and the chalk barrier breached and enlarged with what has been suggested by Gupta et al as a truly cataclysmic megaflood of the English Channel and a widening of the Strait of Dover, eventually making Britain a defined island. A later study by Collier et al of the sea bed of the English Channel has revealed unmistakable features of a megaflood on the English Channel seabed: deeply eroded channels and braided features with remnants of 'streamlined' islands arising from the bedrock among deeply gouged channels where the collapse occurred.

This may have happened during the Late Quaternary period (the last 500,000 – one million years) maybe multiple times as suggested by Mellett et al, and the sea-bed geomorphology was altered by later rises and falls in sea level. It is impossible to date the occurrence of these events during this time period, but they may have been related to temperature fluctuations and the alternating pattern of glacial and interglacial periods. Such megafloods must have re-distributed the pre-existing sand, gravel and shingle moraines deposited by glaciers eons before, as described above, perhaps pushing some of them into shallower coastal sea zones. The consequences of this might help explain some of the next changes in the eastern Sussex coastline in the present known historic era.

Following the LGM the sea level continued to rise and about 8,000 years ago (6000BCE) there was a rise of about 14 metres, until the sea level was only two metres or so lower than it is today. The estimated coastline of eastern Sussex in about 6000BCE is shown in blue in figure 12 below, with the rivers in a dashed lighter blue. By 3000CE the coastline (in dark buff) clearly showed the Wealden and Beachy Head promontories, somewhat larger than in the present day, with the river valleys flooded to become shallow estuarine waters, surrounded by low sandstone sea cliffs.

In addition, as seen in figure 13 the rising sea levels had released vast quantities of shingle, which formed a great shingle bar across Rye Bay, from Pett Level to Old Romney, with mud flats further east. Behind this was formed a large lagoon, sometime

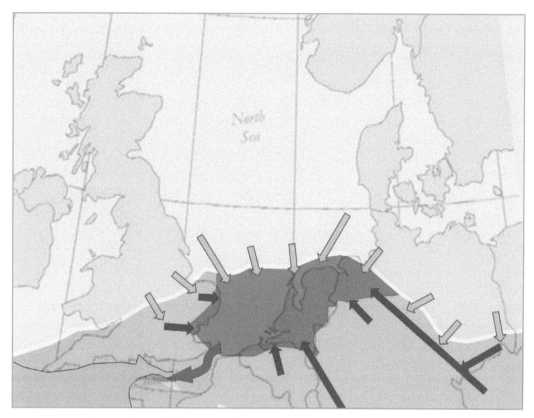

Figure 11. Huge glacier lake trapped between the chalk anticline across the Strait of Dover between England and France and the ice of the Ice Age glacier. The lake filled from melt water of the glacier (light blue) and river water from most rivers of Northern Europe (dark blue). Eventually the water overflowed via the Strait causing a megaflood (red)

Redrawn by Keith Foord after Gibbard, P 'How Britain became an island' in *Nature Precedings* (2007)

called the 'Camera Romaneo' or 'Rye Camber'. Looking east from Fairlight, standing at the top of the high sea cliff just to the east of Hastings, the panorama over Rye Bay and Dungeness would have shown a very big area of a marshy tidal lagoon dissected by 'fleets' of open water trapped behind a large shingle bank (perhaps not dissimilar to Chesil Bank in Dorset). This meant that the old River Rother, then called the Limen, entered the sea near Old Romney rather than at Rye. Later in Roman times its exit was even further east, near Lympne. Williamson highlighted these coastal changes as long ago as 1931 but did not include discussion of any associated sand and shingle movements. Those particularly interested in this should review the superb work of Romney Marsh Research Trust, most of which is available on-line. Their papers on this complex environment are invaluable, as they enable us to understand the historical

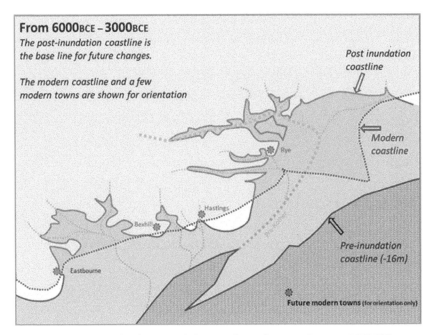

Figure 12. Sea level rises and the coastline of eastern Sussex ©BDHS

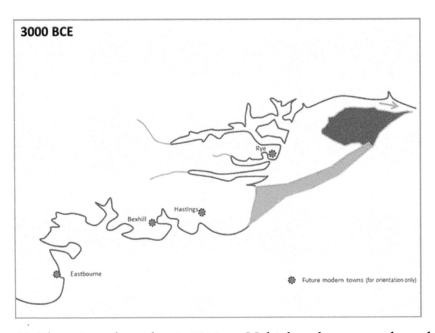

Figure 13. The estimated coastline in 3000BCE. Multiple embayments, a large shingle bar across Rye Bay (yellow) and early mud flats (brown) between the Old Romney and Lympne areas enclosing the 'Rye Camber' or 'Camera Romaneo' with its outlet near Lympne ©BDHS

geographic context of eastern Sussex's and East Kent's former coasts, from Fairlight eastwards. Another interesting read is Ward's paper of 1920 which surprisingly portended the later work.

To the west the Pevensey levels were wide, dry areas in the late Mesolithic/early Neolithic periods, but they became prone to inundations as sea levels rose. By Anglo-Saxon times Pevensey had become an embayed shallow open estuary, dotted with small islands (figure 14), and already its seaward aspect was being partially blocked by shingle banks. The islet areas can still be recognised today as their names are suffixed 'ey' or 'eye'.

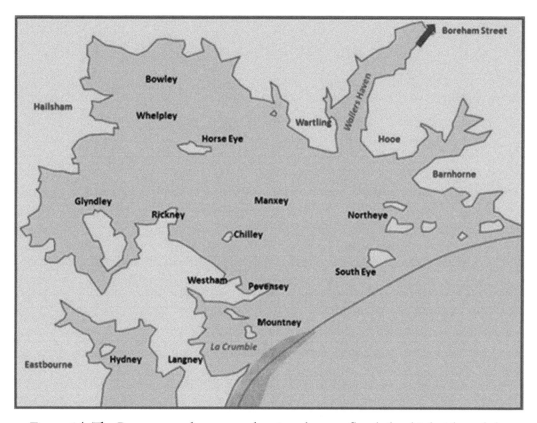

Figure 14. The Pevensey embayment, showing the area flooded at high tide and the small islets (called eys and eyes) with the developing shingle bar off Langney Point. The yellow line shows the present coastline ©BDHS

Another feature left for us to see of the rise and fall of sea levels is the submerged forest at Pett Level, visible at low tides. Here there are three layers of wood peat corresponding to each of the Mesolithic, Neolithic and Bronze ages. When sea levels were low marsh and new forest developed, only to be killed off by saline poisoning from sea water when the sea levels rose again. There is also a small area of Bronze age submerged forest at Bulverhythe, formed in the same way.

Between Bexhill and the present St Leonards-on-Sea lies Bulverhythe (OE. Burgwarahyð – harbour of the people of the burgh) and behind it the Combe Haven valley. The historical geography here is further complicated because of Roman and pre-Roman human activity, silting up the valley. By 800 the coastal outline would have been something like that shown in figure 15. A not dissimilar coast would have presented William the Conqueror with his extended landing sites around Pevensey Bay 266 years later.

All the above is important background data, informing in general terms about the geography of eastern Sussex, and describing the factors which have influenced its coast over the ages, and explaining why the land takes the form that it does today.

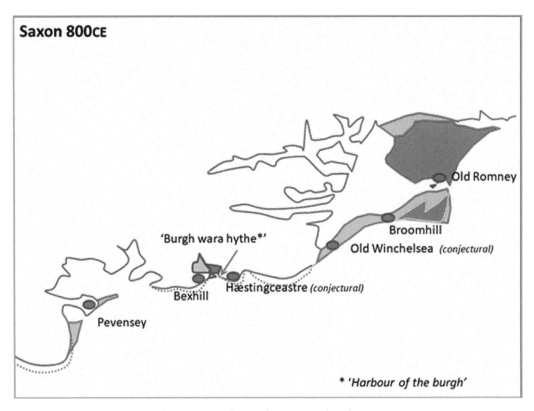

Figure 15. The estimated coastline in mid to late Saxon times.
Headlands had eroded, sand bars were forming across Pevensey Bay, Combe Haven was silted. The shingle bar across 'Rye Camber' or 'Camera Romaneo' was consolidated and settlements evolved at Old Winchelsea and Broomhill. The outlet of the Camera had moved from near Lympne to Old Romney. ©BDHS

What we see today is not what was seen over 1000 years ago. The land and seascapes and ancient harbours have been changed by man, weather and time, and with those changes opportunities and the people changed. Figures 16 and 17 give an impression of how the view may have changed when looking east from Fairlight over Rye Bay.

Some further discussion and interpretations in map form showing the probable changes over the millennia and centuries can be found in *1066 and the Battle of Hastings – Preludes, Events and Postscripts*.

The land and sea remain part of our story today.

Figure 16 . Rye Bay from Fairlight today

Figure 17. The same view with a superimposed interpretation of the spit closing off the wide shallow waters of the Rye Camber (Camera Romaneo)

Photograph and superimpositions © Keith Foord

'Brutus, grandson of Aeneas, beyond the setting of the sun, past the realms of Gaul, there is an island in the sea, once occupied by giants.
Now it is empty and ready for your folk.'

Mythical foundation of Britain from *History of the Kings of Britain*

Geoffrey of Monmouth

2
Early human migrations into south-east Britain: from 12,000BCE until the coming of Rome

As we have seen in the last chapter, no part of Britain would have been a place to live before the end of the LGM without an Inuit-like lifestyle. However, in earlier interglacial periods there is some evidence of intermittent occupation probably by small groups of Neanderthal hunter-gatherers. Evidence of this is very scanty in the eastern Sussex area but some flint and bone finds are recorded.

After that, from about 12,000BCE, migration, with a pause for the Loch Lomond stadial around 10,000BCE, would have started across Doggerland from northern Continental Europe and also via a coastal and sea route from the south-west, in the latter case from south-west France and Basque areas.

It was followed some 6,000–7,000 years later, once agriculture started to be developed, with a further influx of people, not that this influx was huge. Archaeological finds related to this period are commoner on the slopes or higher levels of the Weald, but these are sparser than those found related to the South Downs. But there have been very interesting recent finds related to the Combe Haven valley between Hastings and Bexhill.

Later, from the Bronze Age (1400–600BCE), a bronze working site has been discovered at St Leonards and there have been significant Bronze Age finds in the whole area. This period was a period of rapid social and economic development with a population increase and developing trade networks. By the time the Iron Age started in about 600BCE fortified centres had started to be created. Some have claimed that small hill forts developed on the East and West Hills at Hastings. The only potential evidence for these is an undated bank on the East Hill, but there is nothing definite at all on the West Hill. The ARCHI database records 13 Iron Age site findings within 10km of Hastings, including those related to iron mining and working. Evidence of pre-Roman iron production has been found at Wilting, Crowhurst and Sedlescombe. This iron production was one of the reasons that the Romans became interested in Britannia.

Early migrations and genetics

This late inhabitation means that Britain has a relatively 'simple' early genetic history compared to the complexities of mainland Europe.

Firstly, no genetic differences between the very earliest mainly nomadic *Homo Sapiens* peoples and the first 'later' comers is perceptible. But genetic studies do suggest that all these early peoples have a closer genetic affinity to later Welsh populations than to the later populations of the south-east. There is no evidence, however, that this contributes to a definitive wider 'Celtic' fringe, although there is evidence of more ancient British DNA in common between the Welsh and the north-western and south-western populations of the rest of Britain. Some authors have argued that this derives from a migration around the coast from south-western Europe. This could be possible, but of course, there was to be yet more migration from the adjacent continent to be taken into account, which would change the south-east rather more.

The first sign of this was a new genetic contribution from northern France, post-dating the very original settlers – and curiously this DNA is absent in 'native' north Wales. Apart from this absence, the northern French element is very widely distributed across Britain even to the far north and west. This has been interpreted as representing a very substantial migration, after the very first migrations but well before the coming of Rome.

Today this northern French DNA remains present in the south-east of England's 'native' population at a level of approximately 35% (with a lot of variation). This is not unique, but it is one of the higher levels. The contribution they made and where they came from is shown in figures 18 and 19. By 'native' it should be noted that these DNA samples were taken from people living in rural Britain who had all four grandparents living within 80km (50 miles) of each other. This methodology minimised changes due to the economics-driven population drift related to the late 1800s and to wider immigration changes since then. This study was extremely complex and has been widely reported in both the academic world and in the general press. Other studies have used blood groups, Y-chromosome DNA, maternal mitochondrial DNA, place name and linguistic studies and interpretive studies of cultures derived from archaeological studies. This is becoming a very complex area to study and once the information is fully integrated a fuller picture will certainly appear.

So where did the later 'substantial' migration come from? It is identified by genetic studies, but is not yet fully explained. The author considers that the most likely explanation is that many more people than have been previously suspected kept on coming into Britain, possibly those displaced from the northern French area by population pressure from Franks moving into their territories from further east. Whatever was occurring this was both a large enough and a long enough extended time period of migration – which gradually pushed or drifted northwards, with the new incomers acculturating with the earlier settlers as they went – but not moving into Wales.

This enigmatic finding must refer to something much older and elongated over a more ancient time period than the next migration event which may have started in about 500BCE when early Belgae started to move into southern England.

The maps below are an attempt to show the mainland European origins of the population of the UK, focussing on southern, central and eastern England, using data published by Leslie, S. *et al.*

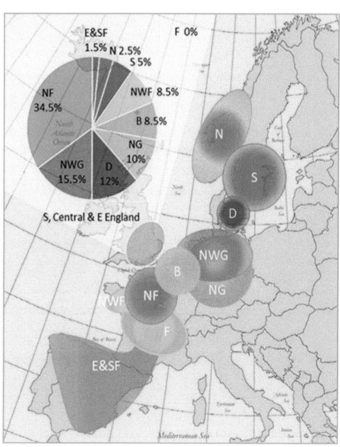

Figure 18. The European origins of the population of the UK. Diagram derived from data published by Leslie, S et al. The zones shown have all contributed genetically. The differing sizes of the zones in this diagram does not correspond to the percentage genetic influence but are indicative of the geographic extent of each zone.
The contributions to Southern, Central and Eastern England only are shown on the inset pie chart. Note that in other areas of the UK the proportions vary.

N: Norway, S: Sweden, D: Denmark, NWG: North-west Germany, NG: North Germany, B: Belgium, NF: Northern France, NWF: North-west France, F: Central France, E&SF: Spain and southern France. This image ©Keith Foord

It should be noted with some surprise that in this large but relatively genetically homogenous area that there is no notable separate genetic contribution from central France, and only small contributions from Spain/southern France and Norway. Northern France, followed by north-west Germany make the biggest contributions, and then northern Germany, Denmark, north-western France and Benelux make up most of the rest .

Figure 19. The area of each square is proportional to the genetic contribution from each source (as in the pie chart in Fig.18) to the population of southern, central and eastern England. Note that this is only for this specific part of England, not the UK as a whole. There is no contribution from central France and only small contributions from Spain/southern France and Norway.

Colours as per previous map. This image ©Keith Foord

Archaeology overview

Many finds were made during the development of the Combe Haven link road between Bexhill and Hastings. Early archaeological information about these finds has been outlined by Champness. 'Evidence was found for activity from four main periods; the earliest spanning the late Mesolithic to Neolithic; followed by the late Neolithic to Bronze Age; late Iron Age to Roman and finally Saxon to Medieval. The Late Mesolithic to Neolithic remains were primarily in situ flint scatters, around the wetland periphery zones of the Watermill and Powdermill Stream Valleys.' 'The scatters may represent four temporary hunting camps and one probable base camp focused on particular topographic locations that potentially provided good vantage points and easy access to the valley bottoms.' Much more will be published about this work in due course.

Many other finds have been made from the earliest periods around eastern Sussex and are recorded in papers in the Sussex Archaeological Collections (SAC), by Hastings Area Archaeological Research Group (HAARG) and others, and listed in the ARCHI database, the East Sussex Historic Environment Record (ESHER – kept at 'The Keep' at Falmer), and the Portable Antiquities Scheme (PAS) catalogues.

Harris describes the archaeobotany of the way in which eastern Sussex, or at least the High Weald zone, became forested – with trees gradually replacing the grasses and shrubs of the immediate post-glacial period. Tree growth started after 9500BCE after the Loch Lomond stadial at first with birch and scots pine, then with hazel (about 8500BCE). Early oak and elm started to appear in about 8300BCE and alder from about 7500BCE, lime (about 7300BCE), ash (about 5800BCE) and beech (about 2500BCE) followed. There was a definite period of severe elm decline in about 4000BCE and the oak which was both tallest and longest lived compared with other tree species came to dominate the Weald.

Figure 20. Drawing of the Mountfield gold ribbed bracelet from *VCH Sussex* Vol.1

Sometime between 1500 and 1100BCE a hoard of gold was buried at Mountfield just north of Battle. Unfortunately, when found in 1863, most of this was illegally melted down, but a fragment of a ribbed bracelet (figure 20) and of a possible plain bracelet are now in the British Museum.

The Coroner's witness report on the treasure trove says that a twisted bar torc, some twisted bar rings and penannular bracelets were also part of the hoard. Gold ribbed bracelets are uncommon in Britain, where most similar items found are of bronze. No explanation as to why this should have been there and to whom the treasure may have belonged has been given.

The Bronze Age appears to have been quite an active period around eastern Sussex. Bowl barrows have been located near

Battle in Petley Wood, at Wellhead Wood, Ewhurst, a ring ditch site at Playden, and recently barrows were identified at Westfield and Ninfield. There was certainly Bronze Age activity in the Combe Haven valley and a Bronze Age trumpet was found when digging a well at Battle some time before 1786. A drawing of this rare cast bronze trumpet of an Irish or Danish type was illustrated by Grose in 1784 (figure 21). We have no dimensions, but these objects are not normally small and are about 60 cm long. Unfortunately, its whereabouts is now unknown. Also found at Battle was a post 1000BCE bronze leaf sword (figure 22). Findings at Cooden and Guestling were palstave axes, at Ewhurst an axe, at Pett and Beckley spear heads and at St Leonards more palstaves and a probable bronze top for a standard pole (figure 23), a dagger on the beach 'between Hastings and Pett' plus at Mountfield a leaf-shaped arrowhead. A Bronze-Age spear was found recently by HAARG near Kitchenham Farm, Ashburnham.

There is also a substantial amount of Bronze Age settlement evidence in Hastings Country Park including a barrow cemetery and a 20m circular Bronze age burial monument, similar to one at Combe Haven, and there are a lot of Bronze Age worked flints there as well. Overall, there is evidence for an active agricultural landscape extending into the Iron Age and Romano-British times, although no significant Roman building has been recorded. An excellent summary report of the country park area has been published recently by Cornwell and Cornwell.

This area as a whole is indeed rich in Bronze Age artefacts.

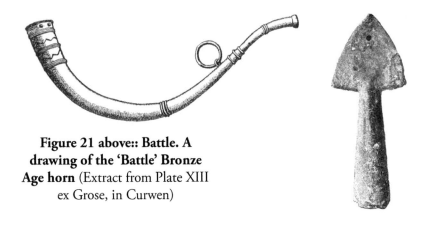

Figure 23. St Leonards. Bronze top for a standard pole (from Evans)

Figure 21 above:: Battle. A drawing of the 'Battle' Bronze Age horn (Extract from Plate XIII ex Grose, in Curwen)

Figure 22. Below: Battle. The bronze leaf sword (re-handled) (from Curwen)

The Eastbourne Area also has an extensive diversity of archaeology particularly the Shinewater Bronze Age settlement, Anglo-Saxon cemeteries and settlement, a Bronze Age round barrow, traces of Iron Age settlement and Neolithic sites. There is a discussion of the Roman villa site here in relation to Pevensey, but It is impossible to include more here, and the interested reader is referred to the publications of the Eastbourne Natural History and Archaeology Society and English Heritage listings for further information.

Belgae

Let us look more closely at the Belgae, as it appears that they had significant influence over southern Britain in pre-Roman times. In about 300BCE our neighbour, then Gaul, was inhabited by various tribes of Celts, but there was also very considerable disparity between those tribes. To the north, Gaul nominally extended across what is now Belgium and into parts of the present Netherlands and Germany, as far as the River Rhine. So, Gaul had Germanic neighbours – or were they all Germanic? There seems to remain a lot of confusion even today about the tribes of a people called Belgae and some evidence suggesting that they were separate from both the Celtic and Germanic peoples, occupying an area between the Rhine, Marne, Seine and the English Channel. This area is shown in green in figures 18 and 19.

They also seem to have spoken a somewhat different language or group of languages from the Gauls. Julius Caesar recorded after 57BCE in his *Commentarii de bello Gallico,* that their language was not the same as the Gauls. He also found them to be difficult foes to conquer – it took him four years between 57–53BCE to do so.

At this time, many Belgae are reckoned to have left for Britain and joined Belgae settlements there. Puzzled Roman writers called them 'distinct Gauls with Germanic ancestry' as a shorthand, and Caesar himself defined Gaul into three parts with Gallia Belgae being the northernmost part. Caesar also tells us the names of numbers of Belgae tribes. Tacitus, whose *Annals* and *Histories* cover the years 14–96CE (that is covering the contemporary time of the later Claudian invasion) said that 'those who inhabited next to Gaul came from Gaul and that between Britain and Gaul the language differs but little.'

Large numbers of Belgae Ambiani tribe coins dating from about 150BCE have been found in south-east Britain. Belgae had clearly migrated into Britain in some numbers (or as others argue had very heavily traded with southern Britain – or maybe both). Belgic tribes in Britain are believed to have been Atrebates, Ambiani, Suessiones, Armorican and the Morini. Frere describes studies of coins and other archaeological material that indicate that there was a large body of Belgic settlers across the whole area from Kent to eastern Hampshire and north to Berkshire, Hertfordshire and Buckinghamshire and suggests that they had become the ruling elite, and extended their influence even further.

Later events suggest that their influence may have extended as far as what became the Fosse Way, a line between Exeter and Lincoln. Figure 24 shows this line and the names of the British Belgae or Belgae influenced tribes, as opposed to British Celtic tribes further north and west. Ellis also records that their coinage has been found slightly further afield – to the Severn–Humber line. Before the Romans arrived the Belgae had created tribal capitals (L. oppida), large areas with huge ramparts and ditches, but there were none in eastern Sussex. The zone, where these and their other smaller forts have been found, also demonstrates their area of activity. One oppidum near Saint Albans enclosed an area of 35ha (86acres). It was from these defensive oppida and because they were strong fighters that Caesar's invasions of Britain in 54BCE and 55BCE were helped to fail.

As always when data is limited debate arises about matters such as how significant

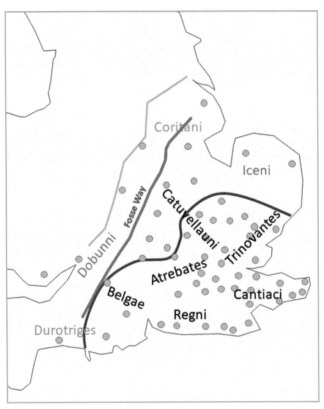

Figure 24. Belgae tribes (in black), their neighbours, the extent of pre-Roman Belgae fortifications (brown line), the Fosse Way line of influence(red) and a simplified indication of the extent and general distribution of Belgae coin finds (yellow).
For a map of more precise locations of coin finds see Oppenheimer, S *The Origins of the British* (2007) p. 332. This map © Keith Foord

were the Belgae in the development of south-eastern England and how extensive were the Belgae territories. There is a reasonable amount of archaeological data to support the above arguments, and it must be certain that the Belgae were strongly represented on the south coast. Caesar wrote that coastal Britain was inhabited by tribes that had earlier migrated from Belgae. One tribe was called simply Belgae, with a capital at Winchester, the Atrebate Belgae were centred on Silchester, in Hampshire, and there were also colonies of Sussione, Armorican and Ambiani Belgae.

But what was the language of the Belgae? It seems to have been linguistically inhomogeneous and may have been a language in transition. Some theories exist around a so-called Celtic/Germanic language interface and it has been suggested that it was the language of the Morini Belgae – a precursor of the west Flemish dialect of Dutch, which had a resemblance to later Kentish Old English, the precursor of which probably came with the Belgae. There continue to be huge linguistic debates about this issue, which will probably never be resolved. Scholars place Old English in the Anglo-Frisian group of West Germanic languages and four dialects of Old English are known: Northumbrian in northern England and south-eastern Scotland; Mercian in central England; Kentish in south-eastern England; and West Saxon in southern and south-western England. In eastern Sussex, partially cut off from the rest of Sussex they probably spoke Kentish Old English.

Celtic place names are rare in the south and east of England and modern English has only a tiny sprinkling of Celtic words. Although this can never be taken as conclusive it is another piece of evidence that any early Celtic language in the south and south-east of England area had been gradually replaced by a language much like Belgic. West and north of the Fosse Way line the language of Britons would have remained a Celtic tongue.

First brush with Rome

Julius Caesar's (figure 25) first reconnaissance of Britain was in 55BCE and not unrelated to his wars against the Belgae, whom he had found had political and military links and support from Britain. Through trading across the western Channel via North-West Gaul the Romans had, it appears, obtained rather more information about south-west England than the south-east and needed to find out more.

Caesar's fleet landed on 26 August 55BCE with two legions, and initially made some progress against the Britons. But they lacked cavalry which had been held up, encountered war-chariots for the first time, and four days later a storm damaged the anchored fleet. This was possibly because the Romans had not taken into account the much larger tidal ranges of the northern seas compared to the Mediterranean. The Britons attacked again but were beaten off and some hostages were taken by the Romans, following which they made a strategic retreat.

In 54BCE the attack was larger, with five legions and 2,000 cavalry in perhaps

Figure 25. Julius Caesar

800 ships (a number almost the same as reckoned for the Norman invasion of 1066). Landing on 7 July Caesar spent two months in Britain and defeated a Belgae confederacy, imposing some terms. He initially forced the Britons back to their oppidum at Bigbury, near present day Canterbury. Again, his ships were damaged, and he spent some time creating a defensive position. This allowed the Britons to rally under the leadership of Cassivellaunus who was probably king of the Catuvellauni Belgae, based north of the Thames. The Britons again employed chariot warfare, to which the Romans were unaccustomed, but they soon devised tactics to counter this and moved on northward, fording the Thames (probably near Tilbury) into Trinovantes territory, and the Trinovantes surrendered. Caesar then swung westwards and came across and took the Catuvellaunian oppidum at Wheathamstead, just north of St Albans, where the Devil's Dyke is a remnant of the oppidum defences. A counterattack by the Britons from Kent against the landing sites also failed and Cassivellaunus gave in. At this point Caesar received news that there were problems in Gaul which required an urgent return, so a deal was brokered, hostages given, and Caesar moved his army back to Gaul to help deal with Germanic invaders.

Following Caesar's attempts to invade Britain Rome fell into some internal disputes and Rome did not contemplate trying again for some time. In the meanwhile the people of Britain continued to develop trading, iron working, settlements and centralisation of elements of ceramic production and to further develop agriculture and consolidation of the tribal kingdoms. They also began to have more trading contact with Rome. This may explain Roman coins dated to this period found at Ashburnham.

This chapter must end with a caveat that genetic studies and linguistic studies of old languages are complex and that the author has just done his best to make sense of what is available and to present it as simply as possible. The interested reader is invited to attempt to unravel the story for themselves, and all should regard the above as a brief overview.

3
Rome, Britannia and the Saxon Shore: 43–409

The central regions of Britain are inhabited by a people who claim to have originated there, on the coast live the immigrant Belgae, who came to plunder and fight, but stayed to cultivate the land.
Tin is found inland and small quantities of iron near the coasts....
In almost all the wars with the Gauls succours had been furnished to our enemy from that country

Julius Caesar

Rome's Britannia project remained in abeyance during a period of significant Roman unrest and stasis of interest. This interest was re-kindled by the Emperor Claudius (figure 26) in 43CE, who 'felt the need' for a military victory. His predecessor, the unhinged Caligula, had played with the idea, but did not get far before he was assassinated in 41. Rome was also eyeing the mineral wealth of Britain, where copper and tin was mined, but particularly the Wealden area where they knew iron working had been established – at places such as Wilting, Crowhurst and Sedlescombe during the late Iron Age (after 50BCE). In addition, Cunobellin, king of the area of the Trinovantes, north-east of the Thames, had recently died and his sons had designs on the Atrebatic kingdom, whose king, Verica, was favourable to Rome. Verica was established enough to produce coinage an example of which was seen in Figure 2. Verica fled to Rome and his usurpation provided another excuse as Roman commercial interest was threatened.

The army landed unopposed around Richborough in Kent. The Britons rallied north of the Medway to try to prevent an advance but were pushed back, probably near Rochester. The Romans

Figure 26 Claudius

then crossed the Thames and headed for present day Colchester. Here the surrender of numbers of tribes occurred and gradually other southern tribes became allied to Rome. The legions gradually pushed forwards to Lincoln and across southern Britain and into the Midlands. Clearly the full occupation took time and there were rebellions to cope with. Many books exist to explain the detail of this, but there is not much written about their activities in eastern Sussex unrelated to their early interest in iron and tile-making, and their later agricultural and fort-building activities related to Pevensey and around Eastbourne. Excavations at Pevensey fort have been extensively reported particularly by Salzman and more recently by Lyne and these were reviewed by Historic England in 2019.

The Pax Romana introduced a network of roads. Locally one extended from the Beauport Park area northwards to Rochester with a branch to Canterbury from near Sissinghurst. Elsewhere in Sussex some extended across the Vale of Sussex from Chichester to Pevensey, from north of which there might have been a link to Beauport via Boreham Street. No definite Roman road directly links south-east Sussex to the nearby Roman shore fort at Pevensey (Anderita, also known as Anderidos in the *Noticia Dignitatum*) which stands on what was a peninsula on the western shore of what was then a large shallow tidal embayment.

HAARG have found elements of a small Roman town at Kitchenham Farm, Ashburnham, near to extensive Roman finds, old Roman saltpans, and a Roman period jetty at the head of Waller's Haven. This was probably a small Classis Britannica port and settlement, dated by CLBR (Classis Britannica) stamped tiles, and significantly pre-dating the fort at Pevensey. They also found part of a metalled Roman road, extending from the old shoreline near Boreham Bridge. This turns and passes under the modern Kitchenham Road (A271). It likely that this may have continued as a high-ground road on the ridgeway though Battle and on to Beauport. Was there also a connection westward to the Roman road from Pevensey that passes through Polegate then onwards towards Barcombe, near Lewes, then westwards? This latter road links up a series of Roman villa farms along the greensand ridge. Interestingly, a later cross-country road along the south coast is shown on Gough's map of 1360 which links Rye, Winchelsea, Battle, Boreham Street (which is specifically depicted and named) and Lewes, with Pevensey lying off-line to the south. Could this follow an old Roman line or just be artistic licence?

The whole Hastings area is slowly being found to have been a crowded, multi-period landscape with continuous occupation and periods of intense industrial activity, which HAARG are helping to reveal. They were also involved, with Oxford Archaeology, in work associated with the Bexhill to Hastings link-road project. One of the findings associated with that was a Roman iron-working site, dated by pottery, at Upper Wilting. This included areas for preparing charcoal, roasting ore and then smelting, with the remains of fourteen bloomery furnaces and hundreds of cubic metres of overlying slag and cinder deposits. This just post-dates the Crowhurst Park iron-working site, which is late Iron Age, dated by pottery.

Evidence for Romano-British settlement has also been found on the ridges of the Combe Haven valley. This suggests that the rural landscape of the early Roman period around Bexhill and Hastings may have appeared quite settled. Deforestation would have been obvious as the furnaces' hunger for charcoal would have been huge.

The Beauport Park iron bloomery between Battle and Hastings was run under military supervision by the Classis Britannica fleet. Its and other furnaces' peak activity was up until about 250, during and just after the northern British campaigns and the construction of Hadrian's Wall. It may also have supplied the Roman legions in Gaul and the wider Roman Empire with iron for weapons as it has been estimated that this was the third largest iron bloomery in the whole Roman empire.

The bathhouse for the ironworks was excavated by Gerald Brodribb in the 1970s, and was re-covered to preserve it, but was noted to be a 'Scheduled Ancient Monument at risk' in 2013. Beauport Park is one of the Romans' lasting industrial memorials and deserves better attention than to be buried under earth and covered with corrugated iron. It is apparently one of the most complete Roman industrial sites ever to have been discovered in Britain and has never been opened to the public. When excavated, the remains were found to contain cold, warm and hot rooms, plunge baths and changing rooms. There are also furnaces, under-floor heating chambers, flues in the walls which channelled heat around the building, and painted plaster which decorated the walls.

The siderite iron ore dug from ore pits (not mines) at Petley, Sedlescombe, Icklesham, Beauport, Bynes Farm, Brede, etc. was smelted with charcoal, and then the crude iron shipped out – northwards via a port run by the Classis Britannica at Bodiam, where there was a Roman settlement which sat at the upper end of a then navigable River Rother, or by a postulated but unevidenced, smaller port at Brede, just north of what appears to be a large iron-processing site. It is likely that the chosen route was downhill which would have made transporting the heavy iron easier. At the nearest small river port the iron was transhipped in barges across the shallow Rye embayment, called the 'Camera Romaneo', to Lympne to be transferred to larger boats. Slightly to the west further bloomeries produced iron which was barged via a small port at Boreham Street at the Waller's Haven headwater of the Pevensey harbour to the deeper waters nearer the mouth of the then harbour for transhipment.

It had been believed that the Beauport site also produced tiles but very recent work by HAARG has found a CLBR tile making facility at Northiam, near the River Rother, downstream of Bodiam. By 2020 a total of 162 complete or partially stamped tiles with the letters CLBR (with variances) had been identified. These have been categorised to 28 different dies which include nine designs that have not been seen before. A magnetometer survey which covered 8.9ha (22 acres) identified two large kilns, within a c.33m x 18m enclosure. Fragments of pots made from the same clay as the tiles have also been found. The remains of a number of buildings have been identified with the largest measuring 38m x 6m. Tiles from this factory, stamped with the Classis Britannica logo of CLBR, made from the local clays, have been found at every CLBR site in Britain and France – except for tiles at Kitchenham Farm and the nearby Castle Croft which pre-dated the above. It may be that the tiles found there were made in situ as recent excavation at Castle Croft found a tile kiln. The Classis Britannica was originally headquartered at Boulogne, with probable later bases at Dover and Lympne (Portus Lemanis).

Bodiam was an extensive Romano-British settlement, lying on the Roman road between Beauport and Rochester just south of the River Rother. The site has yielded quantities of first- to mid-third-century pottery, glassware, coins and tile, scattered over a wide area. CLBR stamped tiles have been found, which has led to the conclusion that the site might have been a major river port of the Classis Britannica.

It is not impossible that some early Roman activity was taking place at Cooden and Barnhorn. ARCHI record a Roman pit plus a possible element of a Roman road and a Roman cremation site at Cooden, although no good written report about this can be found. There are also early indications from the *Sussex Archaeology Round-ups* via the Sussex Archaeological Society website that a housing development at Barnhorn Green is throwing up signs of a late Iron Age/Roman settlement, including a roadway, pottery kilns etc. At the time of writing no further comment can be made.

Margary traced the Roman road from Beauport on the edge of Hastings via Sedlescombe where it passes through the major Roman iron works at Footland and then via Cripps Corner to Bodiam. There, it continues north to near Sissinghurst, then divides, continuing north to Maidstone and eastwards to Tenterden, Ashford and Canterbury.

Roman decline

The Roman Empire in 300–400 was in decline, but Roman interest in the Battle area had declined well before that. The iron-extracting industry moved north-westwards into the higher Weald, possibly as local ore deposits were becoming more difficult to find and the Hastings area had been denuded of timber. The Classis Britannica had also withdrawn in about 250. This dating is evidenced by coin finds from Beauport Park. But this lack of interest is clearly not absolute, and a coin find from Theodosius Magnus (post 353) has been made at Hastings plus other finds from Constantine II (337–340) and his son Constantius II (337–361) have been made. Those of an eastern Roman emperor, Arcadius (395–408) have been found around Pevensey

There were increasing Saxon raids on the vulnerable coast and there were also further perturbations in the Roman hierarchy. The Roman shore fort of Pevensey was the last Saxon Shore fort to be built, in about 293, in response to these complex

Figure 27. Illustration of the command of the Comes Litoris Saxon (Counts of the Saxon Shore) from a 1542–1551 copy of the *Noticia Dignitatum*

The stations depicted are: Othona (Bradwell), Dubris (Dover), Lemannis (Lympne), Branoduno (Brancaster), Garaianno (Burgh), Regulbi (Reculver), Rutupis (Richborough), Anderidos (Pevensey), Portum Adurni (Porchester).

From: http://www. imperium-romana.org/ uploads/5/9/3/3/5933147/ notitia_dignitatum_1542-1551. pdf

factors. As usual there is some uncertainty about its precise role. It has been argued that it was merely a fortified port, but it was built at a time of considerable perturbation in the Roman empire and a time when it is considered that there were increasing Saxon incursions along the south coast. It was also part of a considerable 'Saxon Shore' network under the command of three high-ranking officers (two of whom were based across the Channel in Gaul – something widely overlooked) as figure 28 shows.

By the mid-third century, the Roman navy had also declined. This was during the Roman 'Crisis of the Third Century', between 235–284. The Crisis was a period in which the Roman Empire nearly collapsed under pressures of invasion, civil war, plague, and economic depression. During this period the Classis Britannica vanished under that name, being last mentioned in 249. It is presumed that what was left of it was later subsumed into the Saxon Shore system.

After 283 Diocletian is believed to have re-strengthened the navy and increased its manpower from 46,000 to 64,000 men. After this the Classis Anderetianorum is the only named Roman fleet related to the English Channel that can be identified via the *Noticia Dignitatum*, which although produced in about 400 also referred to earlier periods. This was safely headquartered within Gaul at Andrésy on the Seine (now a western suburb of Paris), not at Anderita/Anderidos (Pevensey). The similar names naturally cause confusion. The fleet's major operational port might have been the river port at Rouen (Rotomagnus), where the Seine is wide. It probably provided transport vessels and some protection from Saxon raiding parties and linked the Saxon Shore forts on both sides of the English Channel. This is a probably simplistic and an unconventional explanation of the naming of the later Classis or events, but it does appear to the author that it is a not inconceivable conclusion and one which was tentatively discussed by Johnson in 1977.

After the reorganization of the empire started by Diocletian which continued into the reign of Constantine the Great, Rouen became the chief city of the central province of Gallia Lugdunensis II and reached the zenith of its Roman development. In this context it should be noted that Gaul was always much more important economically to the Romans than Britannia, which was a troublesome province.

The Channel still needed to be a safe place to trade. In 286 a man named Carausius who had had military success against Gaulish terrorists was given control of a Channel fleet in order to stop raids by Saxons and Franks on the coasts of northern Gaul. But something went very wrong and he ended up in Britannia and was pronounced emperor there and in part of northern Gaul, with the support of several legions. Carausius was assassinated and replaced by Allectus in 293. This was the year that the building of Pevensey fort commenced, which date has ben confirmed by accurate dating of oak foundations under the fort. By 296 Constantius I counter-attacked and Britannia was recovered.

The Rouen area was under the general command of the Dux tracus Armoricani et Nervicani and is also later described in the *Noticia Dignitatum* as 'lying in litore Saxonico' (the Saxon littoral or shore – figure 27). Following the 'Barbarica conspiratio' of 367, when the 'Comes maritime tractus' and probably the 'dux Britannica' were killed, Britannia was again briefly in turmoil and under concerted attack by outsiders. Via a two-pronged seaborn re-invasion via the Solent and the Thames Flavius Theodosius recovered Britannia again. After this it is recorded that the two shores of the English Channel were controlled from both sides by the combined Comes litoris Saxonii, the Dux Belgicae Secunda and the Dux tractus Armoricani et Nervicani (see figure 28). They must have had a fleet available to do this.

The shore fort at Pevensey may have been mainly a trading station and a staging route for large Roman military movements in and out of Britannia, but it also protected the late Roman interests in the Vale of Sussex, between the South Downs and the Weald.

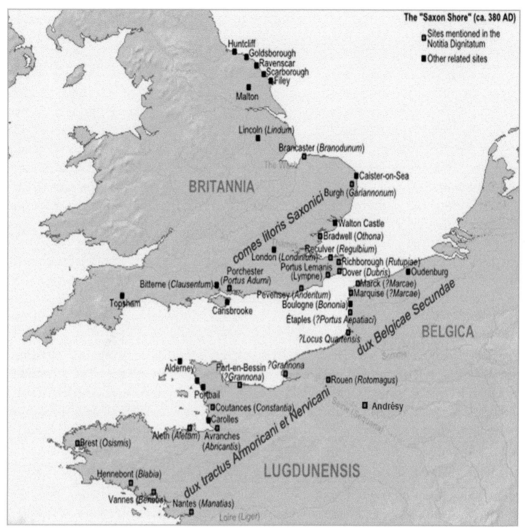

Figure 28. The Late Roman fortifications of the Saxon Shore (Litus Saxonicum) in Britain and northern France

https://commons.wikimedia.org/wiki/File:Litus_Saxonicum.png Ⓒ Public Domain.
Andrésy added

Roman coin finds have been found there, reportedly (in the *Numismatic Chronicle* of 1840) including a hoard containing coins from Constantine I (306–337) to Arcadius (395–408) – an eastern Roman emperor. Kevin Cornwell found a solidus of Arcadius on the eastern edge of Pevensey Levels in the late 1990s. Finds of these last coins suppose a late dating of occupation at Pevensey and suggests that at least some of its garrison may have seen previous service a long way away in the eastern Roman Empire. It was garrisoned by a 'Numeri Abulicorum', perhaps up to 1,000 strong, not a legion but a reserve force of federati (auxillary troops recruited from associated tribes). In this case they were possibly from Abula (now Ávila, between Madrid and Salamanca) in the Hispania Tarraconensis province of Spain. Abulci were also recorded as having seen action in the eastern province of Pannonia Secunda.

In terms of the fortifications of the Saxon Shore, Pevensey fort is an obvious

Figure 29. Grayscale copy of one of Brookes' colour sketches of 1850–51 showing the Eastbourne Villa terrace
From : Sutton, T. The Eastbourne Roman Villa *SAC* Vol 90 (1951–52)

lasting Roman memorial to their local presence. The importance of Pevensey may be accentuated by the known presence of a substantial Roman villa and bathhouse complex only a few kilometres away at Eastbourne, probably pre-dating the fort as a local aristocratic or official residence (figure 29). Possibly partially destroyed well before the fort was built, it might have rivalled the Fishbourne site near Chichester if it had not been almost completely obliterated by a new sea wall and overbuilt. It was described in some careful detail by Dr John Tabor of Lewes in 1717, following its discovery in 1712. In a paper in *Philosophical Transactions* he described a 17ft 4 in x 11ft (5.28 x 3.35m) mosaic floor or pavement and a bath of 16ft x 5ft 9in x 2ft 9in (4.88 x 1.75 x 0.84m) deep, at a level 5ft (1.52m) below the floor. The bath was full of burnt building rubbish and part of a burnt human skull. He also described walls, brickwork etc. and foundations of a long corridor, 225ft (68.6m) long. When next reported in 1743 by Milles the site had been extensively robbed. Wall foundations were noted, although some had been washed into the sea. Further notes have been published and some further findings have been made over the years, with some sketches by Brooke in 1850–51.

The site was almost completely redeveloped and was last seen in 1879. Since then any evidence was either reburied or destroyed by energetic Victorian builders. A small dig was undertaken near Eastbourne pier in 2016 and found a small amount of Roman pottery.

Although there was an inflow of people supporting the Roman administration and military, sourced from all over the Roman empire, this was a relatively small number. Much of an ordinary Briton's life had continued as before, with client kings being tolerated and the development of client kingdoms or civitates to which elements of administration were devolved. The administration in Kent was the civitas of the Cantiaci centred on Canterbury which may well have extended into eastern Sussex as far as north of the Pevensey embayment. Most of Sussex was in the hands of the Regni administered from Chichester.

In time villas for the indigenous aristocracy were built, the nearest definite one to eastern Sussex being at Eastbourne, on the seafront by the pier, as described above. Coin finds at Playden near Rye associated with scattered building material and other objects also imply the presence of Roman activity in the Saltcote Lane area between the A268 and the Military canal. From dating of the pottery and coins, this area appears to have witnessed activity throughout all the Roman period, much like Pett. Playden, somewhat like Pett, would have been a bit out on a limb and on a promontory, so it may have been the site of a signal station or lighthouse, but there is no residual evidence. An alternative would have been something related to salt production, which it certainly was involved in later, hence the nearby Saltcote name.

A coin hoard with coins of Commodus (180–192) and Faustina junior (d.175) was found on the west side of Warrior Square, St Leonards in 1855. Numbers of Roman artefacts, particularly coins mainly with early dates, but some later ones of Constantius II (337–361) have been found around Hastings and a gold coin of Theodosus Magnus (379–395) was found on the beach under the East cliff. Another hoard of Roman coins found off Elphinstone Road, Hastings in 1989 consisted of 53 silver denarii and 92 bronze coins the latest dating from Hadrian (117–138).

There is an unconfirmed report from about 1957 of a few tesserae (the small blocks of stone, tile or glass used to make mosaics) being found near the caravan park on the East Hill, Hastings. This is regarded as a probable hoax as if these had been from a building the East Hill would have been literally littered with artefacts, which it is not. A coin hoard found on the East Hill in 1840 of about 30 coins of Constantine I (306–337) was strangely mixed with some much earlier ones of Hadrian (117–138), this also raises also the possibility of a hoax. It was recorded in a short-lived local paper *The Cinque Ports Chronicle*.

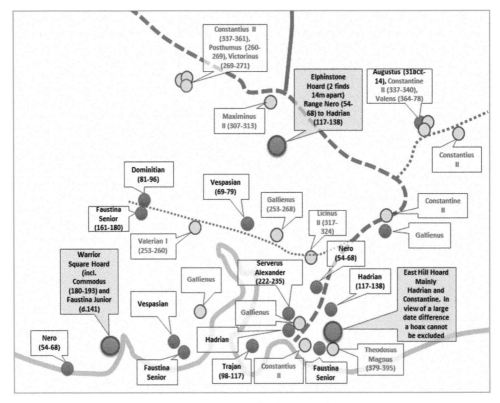

Figure 30. Roman coin finds around Hastings

Pre-250 dated finds are grey circles, post 250 yellow circles all showing emperor or empress names with dating. Large gold circles are hoards. Red lines are tracks, the main dashed track being along the Ridge and descending to the Bourne valley, here there is a cluster of finds. The solid line is the start of the Roman road to Rochester (after Margary). The dotted lines are projected tracks. The blue line is the probable coastline at the time showing an inlet at the Priory valley which may have been big enough to be a usable port. Various sources. Map © Keith Foord

Maps of coin finds from and around Hastings are shown above and below, and they do raise some questions (figures 30 and 31). They suggest continuing low-level activity until late Roman times. As we shall see later, anything more specifically Roman at Hastings may well have been lost to sea erosion, but the author thinks it fair to think that Roman activity around Hastings could not have completely ended when Beauport Park ceased operations in 250. It might have been low key, but it would be interesting to know exactly what it was! Everything is just possibilities and quite enigmatic.

There were changes as time went by, particularly between the first phase of Roman occupation up until the mid-third century and then afterwards with the Diocletian changes to Roman administration. The mid-fourth century saw considerable political disturbances. A minimal very abbreviated history of this is given in the Timeline at the

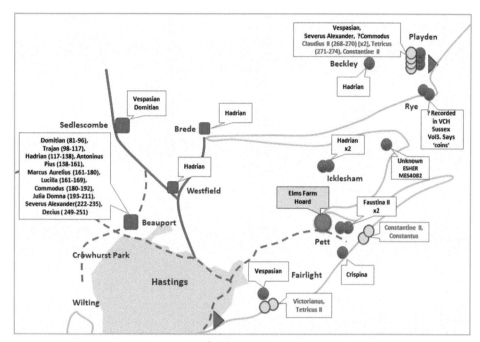

Figure 31. Roman coin finds in eastern Sussex near Hastings
This map shows early and late dated finds as above, and additionally the numerous types of coin found at iron working sites, those with coin finds are representationally shown as blue squares. No late coin finds were associated with these. Possible signal stations as red triangles. Various source.
Map © Keith Foord.

front of this book.

The late fourth century saw a decline of the market economy and industry, and a withdrawal of the Roman military to fight Germanic incursions on the continent, to either support or fight against various usurpers and attempted usurpations of the Empire or parts of the Empire.

The fourth century also saw immigration of Saxon and Frisian settlers into south-eastern England, some of whom became military auxiliaries called federati – numbers of these are recorded as being stationed at Pevensey. These incomers started to ease into positions of power. But because of the relatively low numerical concentration of Roman functionaries, slaves and legions in Britain and the Romans themselves, whilst leaving their built structures, they have left hardly any discernible trace in the overall genetic structure of the British people apart from an interesting small fraction of 1% of African genes.

This tiny amount of African DNA is not unexpected. In 1901 a female skeleton with some African features was found York and was later dated to have lived in the 4th century. In 2014 Eastbourne Heritage Service carried out full analyses of some of the human skeletal remains in their collection, which had come from numbers of mainly

Anglo-Saxon cemeteries. But of particular interest was a female skeleton which had been discovered in 1953 in a probable Roman grave near Beachy Head. This skeleton was confirmed to have been of a woman aged 20–30, who had lived sometime between 125–250 and had grown up in South-east England. She was racially a sub-Saharan African, confirmed by facial reconstruction.

With the departure of the Romans, eastern Sussex suffered setbacks. The iron-making sites had been abandoned long ago; the Roman navy had long gone, and there was civil unrest. Natural decay set in and Saxon attacks and group incursions of Saxon and probably Jutish, Frisian and Frankish settlers increased. The iron-making industry finally collapsed, with only minimal and cruder iron-making in the later Anglo-Saxon period, with no significant revival until medieval times.

In Britain overall, the situation may have been worse in the southern and eastern parts where the Belgic-Britons held sway, compared with Celtic-British areas further north and westwards. It has been concluded by some historians that in Belgic areas the veneer of Roman civilisation was surprisingly thin. Many skills had been lost, due to an overdependence on skilled people and goods imported from elsewhere in the Roman Empire – a lesson with parallels that we should not ignore today.

Fleming's analysis of this time is a somewhat apocalyptic one of severe economic breakdown and sociological collapse, followed by only a slow recovery.

4

Anglo-Saxons and others: who were the Hæstingas?

They first landed on the eastern side of the island, by the invitation of the unlucky king, and there fixed their sharp talon...

Gildas

The period 410–900 is a difficult one from which to find historical data for eastern Sussex. Every now and again someone will ask something like: who were the Hæstingas? Where was Hæstingaceastre? Was there a battle between the Saxons and Romano-Britons near Ashburnham? Did Offa really found a minster church at Bexhill? Where is Hæstingaceastre burghal fort? Could this part of Sussex have been Jutish? When was the Kingdom of Sussex established? When did Sussex become part of Wessex? Did Alfred the Great ever visit Hastings? Etc.

It can be problematic to answer these questions particularly as we find that academic discussion of the Saxon Kingdom of Sussex is nearly always focussed on Sussex between Pevensey to Chichester. This is undoubtedly because this is a somewhat easier zone to study as so much more had been found by archaeologists there. There is truly little direct data from this period from the area between Pevensey and the Isle of Oxney in Kent, otherwise known as Hæstingas.

Just when and why was it first called Hæstingas? To give some answers, we need to go back to the end of the Roman occupation, then follow through the histories of both Sussex and Kent to the time of King Alfred who died in 899. This history is scattered but closer reading of the relevant research and papers that can be found clarifies things a little. This leads to the interesting conclusion that we really need to look much more closely than expected at Kent for influences on the Hastings area. But before proceeding it is worth defining a few terms that will be used.

Acculturation: A relatively modern term used in historiography to describe the results of contact between two or more different cultures. From these composite cultures emerge, in which some existing cultural features are combined, some are lost, and new features are generated.

Angles: A group from the south of Denmark and adjacent areas of Germany

Cantiaci, Regni, Trinovantes, Belgae, Atrebates and Catuvellauni: These refer to the pre-Roman tribal areas of south-east England. In these areas they probably spoke variants of Belgic and were closely related to the Belgae of northern Gaul.

Embayment: The description of a wide area of coastal low-lying land that becomes inundated following a sea level rise, forming a large shallow bay.

Franks/Frankish: Germanic people who lived in the region of the lower and middle Rhine, Netherlands and Belgium. They later merged with northern Gauls and formed the kingdom of Neustria. Modern France takes its name from these people. Some Franks migrated into Kent and possibly eastern Sussex from about 500 onwards.

Frisians: These were also a west Germanic people, from the North Sea coastal areas of Netherlands and Germany. Old Frisian is a close cousin of Old English, Kentish Old English is believed to derive from Old Frisian.

Hide: A unit of land area originally intended to represent the amount of land sufficient to support a family. Depending on the quality of the land it could measure between 25-50Ha (60 –120 acres).

Jutes/Jutish: These peoples probably came from Jutland in present day Denmark. They were associated with the Frisians from the North Sea islands off Denmark, Germany and the Netherlands and may themselves have originally moved to Denmark from the Baltic shores of what is now north Germany.

Romano-Britain/British: This refers to the land and people of the Roman province of Britannia at the end of and for some time after the Roman occupation, the end of which is normally dated 409CE. This terminology is used as the British had adapted to Roman ways. The length of time the population remained 'Romano-British' after the Romans left varies according to where in Britain they lived, so the further they were away from Saxon, Angle and Jutish incomers the longer they could be termed Romano-British. Once fully acculturated with the incoming Germanic peoples the term English can start to be applied to the people within the whole area now known as England.

Saxons: A larger group, from a zone lying between the Angles and Franks, but extending much deeper south-eastwards into Germany.

–wara(e): As a word ending means 'people of'. Alternatives are '–ge' (used somewhat earlier) and '–ingas' (usage 600 onwards). An example is Cantwara for the people of Kent.

And a word about some spellings: A mixture of Roman (Latin) prefixed L., 'Old English' prefixed OE., and modern place names is used throughout this book. Spellings can vary as they are copied from original spellings which were variably recorded. Some OE. letters are used such as þ and ð both = th, þ pronounced more like the 'th' at the start of 'the' ð as at the end of words as in 'oath' ; ſ = long s ; æ = short a as in 'cat' but before an r or with an acute accent ǽ it is more like 'ai' ; œ= like a short e, except if followed by another vowel when it is long; h is always pronounced at the beginning of a word, even if the next letter is a consonant.

Acculturation changes

The tribal patterns of pre-Roman Britain had not been altered by the Roman occupation, but there had been some Romanisation of the upper echelons of the Britons. After the adoption of Christianity by the Romans there was some late Christianisation in Britain, more in the north and west than in the south, although this may not have been embedded as deeply as in neighbouring Gaul. Latin or a variety of it called generically Vulgar Latin had been used in towns, for administration, by the elite and army, but in south-east England the common folk retained their Belgic tongues. The people could however be collectively called Romano-British and initially, for 50 years (or even up to 100–150 years in places further to the north and west, where people were Romano-Celtic and not Romano-Belgae) some variable veneers of Rome persisted.

This was clearly a time of complex changes. To understand these requires a combined application of oral and early written histories, archaeology, geographic history, linguistic history, place-name studies, and early literature to reconstruct exactly what happened – and this must have varied considerably between different localities. As Higham said when discussing the transition from sub-Roman Britain to Anglo-Saxon England

'We should neither assume massive continuity nor massive discontinuity.'

The south-east coastal areas of Britannia had already admitted some Germanic peoples, notably Saxons, Frisians and Jutes, to come and settle before the end of the fourth century, and it should be noted that the final Roman legions and federati were also partially drawn from such folk. These had already acculturated to a degree with the local people and those who 'stayed on' added some continuity and stability.

Modern historical thought is that the early post-Roman Anglo-Saxon incomers, also Germanic, were rather more influenced to immigrate by this relatively short (perhaps only lasting one or two generations) period of post-Roman stability than might have been expected. This contrasts with the traditional history that 'barbarians' came in and killed or chased out the Romano-British in an historic ethnic-cleansing operation.

The effect of Germanic settlement is considered by some historians to have been significantly stronger in the very south-east, in Kent and Essex (and also eastern Sussex/Hæstingas?) where the Cantiaci-Romano-British and the Trinovantes-Romano-British respectively lived and spoke languages which had similar linguistic roots to the incomer's language. The theory also suggests that these groups were in general more exposed to northern Gaulish cultures and perhaps more heavily 'Romanised' than those further afield.

Where Germanic tribes had settled, their presence catalysed or 'aided' the further changes about to occur. The Romano-British structures gradually broke down over a generation or two, but some sort of sub-Roman organisation persisted with local 'kings' appearing. One called Vortigern, perhaps some sort of High Lord or Overlord of the area of southern post-Roman Britannia, possibly originated from Gwent – it's all a bit vague – and his council invited some 'Angles' (more likely Saxons and/or Jutes) into the territory of the Cantiaci, which had retained a significant Romano-British culture, to help with holding off the attentions of other less desirable tribes from across the North Sea. This group arrived around Ebbsfleet near Ramsgate, sometime before 450, led by the near mythical Hengist (aka 'Stallion') and Horsa (aka 'Horse'). Gildas spikily refers to their original settlement as on the 'east side of the island ... and there fixed their sharp talons'. Nennius clarified that this first settlement was on the Isle of Thanet and records the year as 447. Archaeological discoveries on Thanet have supported the presence of an early Germanic settlement there. Gildas, a moralist, not an historian, judged Vortigern to have been careless and lacking foresight and called him 'unlucky', which was in fact very mild for Gildas. In Kent the aggression which started to occur in about 450 came from these 'invited' incomers, who clearly liked what they had found and wanted more of it. At first their activities were mainly in north and west Kent. East Kent may have had a gentler time due a concurrent influx of Jutes and Frisians – who would later have a major influence in forming the local regnal families.

Hengist and Horsa, the leaders of the 'invitees', and their men had at first helped fight off 'the Picts' (probably the generic name given to anyone from 'the North'), but observing that the land was good and their hosts weak the news soon got back home. More Saxons, Angles, Jutes and Frisians slowly arrived. Hengist and Horsa then fought the local Romano-British at Aylesford (Kent) in about 455. Horsa was killed and replaced by Oisc (aka Œric or Æsc), son of Hengist, from whom the later kings of Kent took their family name 'Oiscingas' (people of Oisc).

The next year there was another battle with the Romano-British at Crayford, with the Romano-British losing and their leaders retreating to London which remained a safer haven. Following this still more immigrants arrived into Kent. Nine years later Hengist and Oisc were penetrating deeper into Britannia and in 465 another battle took place at Wipped's Creek (an unknown location, possibly in present day Surrey or north Hampshire) with the death of a dozen British chiefs. A further battle in 473 sent the Belgae Romano-British leaders fleeing – presumably to the north and west, where the Celtic Romano-British had retained a stronger hold, but it was unlikely that there was any mass displacement or ethnic killing of the indigenous general population in the south and east. Clearly the remaining folk would have found themselves subjugated to new Anglo-Saxon lords (figure 32).

The implication of all this is that the 'action' was in north Kent, with the invaders then driving deeper into Surrey and north of the Thames, engaging the Atrebate and Catuvellaunian Romano-British. This may well have left east and southern Kent relatively open and more peaceable people arrived, mainly Jutes, possibly with some Frisians and Franks, who settled and started to acculturate with the remaining Cantiaci, who still probably spoke a Belgic language not dissimilar to the Germanic languages of the incomers. The Jutes were able to establish a 'kingdom' in east Kent, which acculturated with the residual Romano-British culture. They also remained, at least initially, influenced by Frankish culture from across the sea.

Kent, the kingdom that was formed by the Jutes, appears to have extended beyond what is Kent today and incorporated the traditional territories of the Cantiaci, which as well as including all of Kent, included eastern Sussex (i.e. Hæstingas), eastern Surrey and London south of the Thames. This implies that the Hæstingas area may have had a rather more Cantiaci Romano-British and Jutish/Frisian/Frankish Kentish history than the rest of Sussex which was Regni Romano-British then South Saxon.

Chevallier suggested that there had been some north Frankish influence on the Hæstingas, a view generally supported by other historians. However, the Jutes appear not to have ventured much further into Sussex, perhaps satisfied for the moment with their holdings, perhaps somewhat deterred by the aggressive South Saxons and disappointed with the poor soils around what would become Hæstingas. Some voyaged down the coast and settled in the Isle of Wight and around the Solent (becoming known there as the Wihtwara and the Meonwara respectively).

On Hengist's death Oisc became King of all Kent in 488. During his time some early Franks arrived from northern France, being accepted via aristocratic marriages. Their influence is shown in grave goods. In about 560 King Æthelbert of Kent married Bertha, a daughter of the Frankish king of Neustria, the new western Frankish kingdom, west of the Meuse and north of the Loire.

Because some areas were further from the central influence of their 'kingdoms' than others sub-regions developed. In the south of Kent one of these was called Limenwara. In Kent there are present day echoes of the boundaries of this Kentish 'lathe', in the area now called Shepway, in south Kent. When this was first mentioned in approximately 700 it was named after the Limen River (the precursor of the River Rother which later changed its course and would later still be part of the defined boundary between Kent and Sussex).

The local Limenwara formed an early administrative subdivision of Kent to the east of Hæstingas, although the Limenwara may never been as 'independent' as the Hæstingas. The name means 'people of Limen'. It was based around two main settlements, with Lympne as the original centre of administration and Lyminge as the territory's minster and centre of ecclesiastic administration.

According to its foundation myth, Sussex was invaded slightly later than Kent,

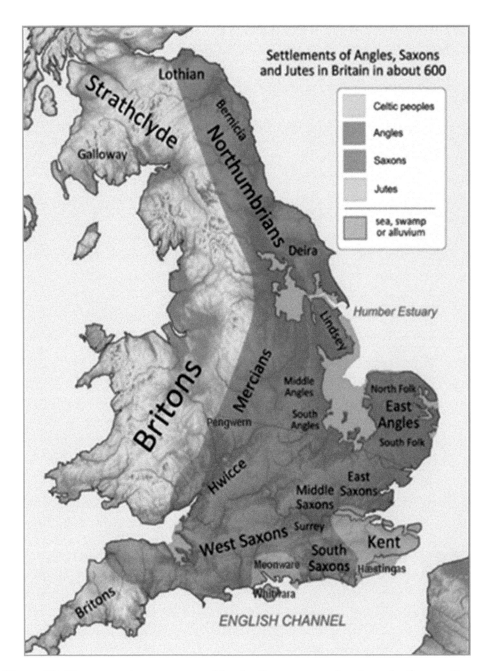

Figure 32. The approximate extent of Anglo-Saxon expansion into the former Roman province of Britannia, by about 600. Hæstingas is shown as an extension of Kent and Meonwara, Wihtwara and Pengwern are identified

Modified with the addition of Hæstingas and the naming of Pengwern, Meonwara and Wihtwara from Wikimedia: https://commons.wikimedia.org/wiki/File:Britain_peoples_circa_600.svg, "Britain peoples circa 600" CC by sa /3.0.

and from its west – after 477 by Saxons (led by someone who may have been called Ælle) rather than Jutes. Spreading east from around Selsey they took a while to reach Pevensey with its residual Romano-British stronghold based on the Roman Saxon-Shore fort. The coastal plain of west Sussex and the Vale of Sussex between the Arun River and Pevensey must have been attractive agriculturally to the 'South Saxons', but east of Pevensey the more difficult sub-Wealden terrain of Hæstingas, trapped between two large tidal embayments with their extensive mud flats, the coast and the Wealden forest (OE Andredes leag), would have been less attractive (figure 33). The Saxons may have also met some early resistance from Jutes who had already migrated to there from Kent. The story of the Saxon invasion of the Regni territory goes like this: described in the ASC for 477:

> Here Ælle and his three sons Cymen, Wlencing and Cissa came to Britain with three ships at the place which is called Cymen's Shore (OE. Cymenes ora, probably 'The Owers', a sandbank off Selsey) and there killed many 'Welsh' (i.e. Romano-Britons) and drove some into the wood which is named the Weald (OE. Andredes leag).

Until 485 it was so far so good for the people who lived in what would be called Hæstingas sometime in the future, who were a little distant from the wilder events of north Kent and would have only been slowly introduced to any newcomers. But Ælle then turned eastward…

> Ælle fought against the Welsh (the Romano-British) near the margins of Mearcred's Burn.

So, by 485 we get to a small conundrum centred around 'Town Creep' a small area which lies off the B2096 road from Battle to Netherfield. This may be the site of the nebulous Battle of Mercredsburn, [OE. Mære (boundary) + OE. Burhna (stream)]. If this happened could it have indeed been a border fracas between the South Saxons and the Kentish Romano-British allied with their new Jutish neighbours, the boundary being deemed the small river called Wallers Haven, which enters the north east of the Pevensey Levels, and its tributaries? The villagers of Ashburnham and Penhurst in East Sussex have an oral history that a pre-Saxon earthwork rather oddly known as Town Creep, situated in Creep Wood which adjoins the two villages, was the site of Mercredsburn. Oral tradition surviving to the end of the 19th century referred to the earthwork as being the site of a town which was besieged and destroyed by the Saxons. Even today a 'Penhurst Harbour' is referred to by Penhurst residents. In 1896 a member of the Sussex Archaeological Society investigated this claim, and subsequently published a paper concluding that the earthwork was a possible old Roman way fort and the location for the battle of Mercredsburn, that the name 'Creep' could have an etymology derived from the latter part of 'Mercrede', whilst the 'burn' (or stream) may refer to the Ashburn stream (a tributary of Wallers Haven) running nearby. Later the theory was somewhat peremptorily discounted, but the rumours still rumble. Today Creep Wood is managed woodland and the features previously discussed by Tatham and Napper are obliterated. Although it is not impossible to imagine from the contour maps, which indicate a small steep sided plateau, confirmed by a small group visit from BDHS in 2017, that it could have been a very strategic site, with a view all the way down the valley to Pevensey, future formal investigation is unlikely. In any case Welch (in Brandon) suggests that the Mercredsburn could have been one of the Ouse or Cuckmere rivers, west of Pevensey, so the claim that it is Waller's Haven/Ashburn stream is debatable. The outcome of this battle is undefined, just like its site. Six years later the ASC records that in 491 the South Saxons turned on the Romano-British at Pevensey and wiped out the defenders... it says:

> Here Ælle and Cissa besieged Anderitum and killed all who lived in there; there was not even one Briton left there.

Hæstingas is first mentioned at about the same time as the Limenwara (above), i.e. 700, but it is probable that both discrete areas pre-dated this by a century or two, even if not with quite the same names. It has also been suggested, in studies of place

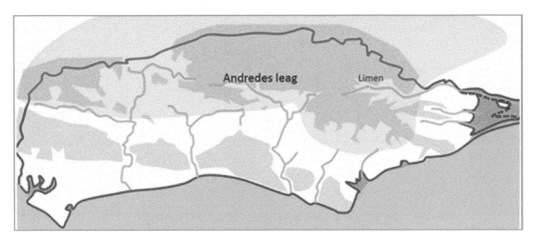

Figure 33. Base map of Sussex in about 800
Showing the tidal embayments at Chichester, Selsey, Pevensey, Bulverhythe and Romney (the huge 'Rye Camber') plus the large shingle bank on which Old Winchelsea would stand. Shown are main rivers, land over 60m (200ft) in green and the possible extent of the Andredes leag overlaid in buff. Note that the River Limen (later the Rother) at that time flowed eastwards north of the Isle of Oxney and entered the sea near Lympne in Kent.   Map©BDHS

names, that the earlier the name the more likely it was that the name of a person rather than a geographical locale would be used as the prefix, if so Hæstingas on these grounds would have pre-dated Limenwara.

The centre of Hæstingas must have been Hæstingaceastre, the site recorded just before 900 as an Alfredian burghal hidage fort, and where Athelstan later set up a mint in 928. Gardiner and others have discussed at some length the probable position of Hæstingaceastre. The analysis of the scanty available information suggests that the fort or fortified settlement stood somewhere west of the present town centre of modern Hastings and has been completely lost to the sea by cliff erosion. The possibility that Hæstingaceastre could have been Pevensey Castle gets raised occasionally but does seem very unlikely. The author believes the idea can be discarded on etymological grounds alone.

Burghal forts were established in the late ninth century as English defences against Viking raids, and were part of the Alfredian strategy to recover all of England from the Danes, with the coastal forts designed to deter further Viking raids. The burgh of Hæstingaceastre had the income and support of the people of the 500 hides (94 sq. miles/243 sq.km) of productive land attached to it. This area is perhaps about 50% of the total area of Hæstingas, so would correlate well as the other 50% would have been non-productive forest/marsh etc.

The total wall length around all the burghal forts can be correlated to their supporting hidage and so for Hæstingaceastre is estimated to have been about 625m (2060ft). If the fort was square each wall would have been about 160m long and the contained area about 2.5ha (6acres). If the southern boundary was a cliff face (as seems likely for Hæstingaceastre) it may have had a larger area. Often the OE word 'ceastre' meant not a just a castle or fort, but a town enclosed by an earthen wall topped with a timber stockade or stone wall. Therefore, Hæstingaceastre would mean the stockaded town of Hastings (or rather the precursor of the newer town which would develop later in the Bourne valley east of the hill on which the ruins of the Norman castle now stand).

The natural boundary for the Hæstingas sub-region, whether as an outlier of Kent or of Sussex, in the earliest days must have been in the west from a point north of the extensive Pevensey Bay embayment, eastwards possibly as far as the Limen (Rother) river which at that time flowed north of the Isle of Oxney, and to the north the Wealden forest (figure 34). It is also noted that there is a Hastingford (across the River Uck) just north of Hadlow Down and south of Crowborough (38km/24miles from Hastings) and Hastingleigh (leigh = clearing or meadow) just southeast of Ashford in Kent (64km/40miles from Hastings), which might indicate the 'influential range' of Hæstingas. The name Hastingford suggests a planted community, maybe in the late seventh century. The first recorded spelling for Hastingleigh (in 993) was Hæstinga lege.

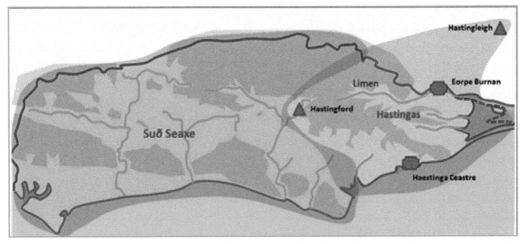

Figure 34. The possible early zone of influence of the Hæstingas, at the eastern end of Suð Seaxe, stretching into Kent ©BDHS

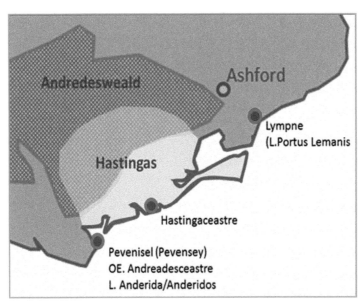

Figure 35. The possible coastal and Wealden extent of Hæstingas territory ©BDHS

Berry points out that neither archaeological finds nor place-names provide evidence for much early settlement in Kent south of the North Downs and that the modern Hastingleigh in Kent may be a relic of a clearing in the once extensive forest as an outlier of Hæstingas.

We can therefore postulate that Hæstingas was a 'buffer zone' between the South Saxons to the west and the somewhat more developed Jutish Kingdom of Kent to the east (figure 35). Sussex itself at times was a divided 'kingdom' and sub-kings for east and west are sometimes recorded. Even today it seems a long way from Rye to Chichester, along a difficult road or a discontinuous railway and Sussex has been administratively divided into East and West counties. The long thin nature of Sussex does not lend itself to rapid physical communications or political unity and the early South Saxons were possibly held at bay as undesirable neighbours by Kent, particularly as the former had brutally sacked Pevensey.

So what else has been found, inferred and theorised about 'Hæstingas', Kent and Sussex in that long grey period 450 – 900? The following is based on truly scanty evidence (or as Brandon says, near transparent evidence; another colleague calls it 'flexible logic') particularly with regard to Sussex and even more so for Hæstingas, and somewhat from Kent, but we shall try to focus on where Hæstingas fits into the story. After all, as Reaney concluded:

> people whose individuality could be remembered for some 500 years and who, at the end of that period, could be mentioned in a national chronicle side by side with the people of Kent and the South Saxons, must have been more than a mere fragment of a larger kingdom.

Sussex Archaeological Society sagely notes on its website that the written record is not reliable and archaeological evidence, particularly burials, has provided the main evidence of where the early Saxons settled in Sussex. Saxon cemeteries have been found at Alfriston, Selmeston, Bishopstone, Beddingham, Glynde, Saxonbury (Lewes) and Woodingdean. The Anglo-Saxon objects displayed in the ground floor gallery at Barbican House Museum in Lewes are from some of these sites.

Myres postulates that Sussex became somewhat fragmented in Saxon times into zones divided by the rivers that flow north to south and cut through the South Downs. Because of this there was no natural centre, and Roman Chichester soon became relatively unimportant, with Pevensey fort becoming a major defensive centre at the end of the Roman period and onwards into Romano-British times. He suggests that its importance was such that it eventually gave its Roman name to the Wealden forest as the OE Andreadsweald. We also know that the coastal plain of west Sussex and Vale of Sussex, between the South Downs and the Weald had been well settled by the Romans and Romano-British and that there was a network of roads linking farms and villas in mid-Sussex as far east as Eastbourne villa and Pevensey Roman fort, so the terrain should have been easy to cross.

Many place names in Sussex are Saxon names, the Saxons having settled the lowlands of Sussex and named most of what we see today, but there are clear place name frequency differences going from west to east, which could additionally indicate poor penetration of the South Saxons eastwards of Pevensey. For example, place names including 'hamtun' are only found in the west of Sussex and are unknown in Kent. In

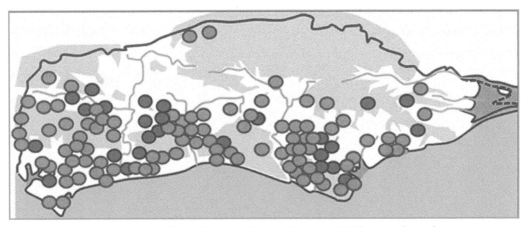

Figure 36. Distribution of 'tun' (tan circles) and 'ingtun' (blue circles) place names in Sussex. Note a relative sparsity of such names within the Hæstingas area (modified from *Historical Atlas of Sussex*)

the Hæstingas area there are more 'ham(m)' names than 'tun' names, much more so than in the rest of Sussex to the west. A map of place names ending 'tun' and 'ingtun' is shown in figure 36.

It is wise not to rely too much on place-names – but we are fortunate that in 1086 *Domesday Book* left largely unchanged the pre-1066 English place names (although sometimes not very accurately). This gives us a residual old southern England place-name history and 'ing' or 'ings' containing or ending place-names are very common in the Hæstingas area. 'Ing' has been shown to refer to 'a place associated with' which can be a person, people or a local feature, (e.g. Wartling – place belonging to Wyrtele). Whilst this sort of 'ing' name points to early sixth-century settlement (Stenton), 'ing' names were still being formed later, so we must take care with analysis. 'Ingtun' and 'ingham' names were slightly later names (e.g. Whatlington – farm or settlement of Hwætel's people; Kitchenham – Cyssi's home or enclosure) possibly formed from the seventh century onwards. It should also be noted that this was not the case everywhere in Britain. In eastern England names like 'ingham' were also associated with the Angle's pagan god Ing, otherwise known as Freyr, twin brother of Freyja.

There is also a profusion of 'ham' names, such as 'Uckham' rather more towards Kent than to Pevensey. Village.net records localising 17 'ing/ings' names, nine 'ingtun/ ingham' and 37 'ham' names in the Hæstingas area alone. Figure 37 below left includes most of the 'ham' names plus some additions. Stenton also notes that both the place names and field systems of Hæstingas have affinities with Kent, again suggesting but not proving influence from or of colonisation from Kent.

Of course, the big question is the origin of the name Hæstingas itself. The 'ingas' form is subtly different from 'ing' and means 'people of' which could be named after a tribe or place and may be a later suffix than '-ge' or '-wara' (as in OE. 'Surridge'

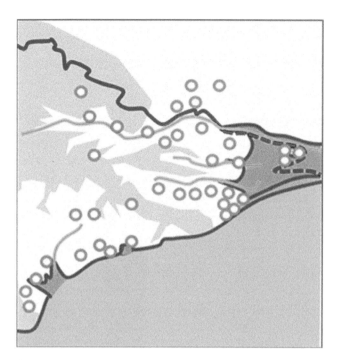

**Figure 37.
Prominence of
place names ending
in 'ham' in the
Hæstingas area**

(Surrey) or 'Limenwara') which both also meant 'people of'). So 'Hæstingas' is an OE word meaning settlement of Hasten's or Hæsten's people. Hæsten would have been a (to us unknown) local chieftain or sub-regulus, possibly extant circa 600. The nearest translation of OE. 'hæste' means 'raging' or 'violent', so the name does not help us to decide if it was a real name or nickname, one can suspect the latter. But whatever Hæsten's etymology Hæstingas as an entity must have existed before 710, when we have the first recorded version of the name – so possibly it had existed for a century or two. Hasten the Viking as mentioned in the ASC(A,E) for 892–894 is clearly a total red herring for giving a component to the name as he lived nearly 200 years after Hæstingas is first recorded.

The Kingdom of Sussex was originally OE Suð Seaxe meaning the land of the South Saxons, but the kingdom seems to have remained fragmented and vulnerable to outside power struggles. From 495 onwards yet more Saxons arrived further to the west and started to take over parts of Hampshire north of the Meonwara Jutes (who lived around the Solent). They pushed northwards, fighting the Atrebate Romano-British of the Thames valley area at Salisbury in 552 and eventually forming the kernel of the Kingdom of the West Saxons –Wessex. This was a little far west to affect Hæstingas at this time – except to note that in 568 Wessex undertook an aggressive expansion mainly to the west and north and had expanded north of the Sussex Weald into Surrey, forcing the Jutish Kingdom of Kent back into its home territory. This event is the first recorded conflict between two groups of incomers (i.e. Saxons and Jutes), rather than a battle by Germanic invaders against the Romano-British. The location of this conflict was Wibbandun, which can be translated as Wibba's Mount, but the site has not been clearly identified. Of course, if the folk memory of the Battle of Mercredsburn is correct this might have been the very first unrecorded conflict between the Saxons and Jutes.

Between about 514 and about 600 South Saxons are curiously absent from mentions in any records until in 607 the West Saxons under Ceolwulf fought a campaign against them. The result is however unrecorded. Later 'kings' of Sussex do not claim descent from any of Ælle's sons and a century and a half later other families had risen to prominence. It is from these that the kings were selected. Unfortunately, no fully authentic king list remains for Sussex and the 'kings' may in any case have ruled in groups of up to three or four at a time, with power being shared between them.

It appears undoubted that a new sociological structure emerged from the ingress of the Anglo-Saxons over a long acculturation period. Unfortunately, this led to an apartheid-type society controlled by the dominant Anglo-Saxons. Even amongst slaves, people of Briton origin were regarded as of lower status than Anglo-Saxon slaves. Evidence of the apartheid system can be found in the 7th century laws of Ine. For example, these laws stated that if an Anglo-Saxon was killed, the wergild (blood money) payable to the person's family was up to five times more than the fine payable for the life of a native Briton. The ratio and amount were also highly dependent on the status of the individual and whether they were 'free' or not. There is also a later parallel: Härke has noted:

> The ethnically divided post-immigration society of early Anglo-Saxon England where the natives had an inferior legal and social status even though they were in the majority, is closely mirrored in the post-Conquest society created by the Normans in England after 1066.

Not all Britons became slaves and at all levels there was intermarriage and surely many liaisons. Few Britons can have wished to remain in a distinct inferior ethnic group and the populations gradually merged.

The Anglo-Saxons certainly influenced the genetic structure of Britain, particularly across a wide eastern, central and the southern zone of England. These major Anglo-Saxon genetic contributions come from individuals who had origins from north and north-west Germany and from Denmark. However, the proportion of such ancestry cannot be pinned down to a specific percentage – it has a range of 10 to 40%, but the median proportion in south-east England is about 22%, of which 10% is German and 12% Danish. This represents an extensive addition from the dominant incomers to the native British mix which has been described in previous chapters.

5
The kingdoms of south-eastern England until the death of Alfred in 899

In 766 Offa came to the Mercian throne and ... decisively subdued the kingdoms of the south-east ... subjugating the South Saxon kingdoms and reduced their kings to mere duces, and in 771 also conquered the Hæstingas at the eastern end of Sussex.
Drewett, Rudling and Gardiner, 1988

Figure 38: The centre of the Alfred Jewel
From: https://archive.org/stream/dressesdecoratio01shaw_0#page/n30/mode/1up

In about 661 a first reference to a sub-king Æthelwalh of Sussex is found, from brief mentions in Eddius's *The Life of Bishop Wilfrid*. This was in the same year that Wulfhere of Mercia had gained control of Sussex. Æthelwalh was possibly a younger son of Cynegils of the West Saxons, although quite how he became 'king' of Sussex is unknown. We are told that Wulfhere 'made' him marry Eafe, daughter of the

Christian King Eanfrith of the Hwicce and to accept baptism. The relevance of this is that the South Saxons were among the last to convert to Christianity from paganism. According to Bede's history they had remained stubbornly "heathen" until very late in the seventh century.

Christianity arrived some 100 years later in Sussex than in Kent and it was only after Sussex had a maybe somewhat reluctant Christian king and after the founding of Selsey Abbey in 681 that Christianity truly took root. Hæstingas might have remained pagan somewhat longer than western Sussex, but the influence of the nearer and stronger Christian Kent based at Canterbury might have had the opposite effect .

Kent had retained its etymology from the original pre-Roman Cantiaci and retained recognisable Romano-British city names (e.g. Canterbury from Cantiacorum, Dover from Dubris). This was unlike all the other kingdoms of Britain which almost completely lost links with their Roman names. Kent also had a more elaborate culture than other English settlements and there were some continuing connections with the Franks of north-west Europe, who had had a more enduring Christian presence, possibly because it had been more firmly established in late Roman times than in the more peripheral Britannia. But a very strong Frankish influence is not supported by linguistic evidence nor by the fact that Kent remained pagan until St Augustine arrived in 597. The Frankish princess Bertha had married King Æthelbert of Kent in about 560, and brought a Frankish bishop with her, but this did not bring about an immediate mass Christian conversion.

After 597 Augustine established an archbishopric near Canterbury. He was allowed to worship at the small surviving Romano-British church of St Martin's, before founding a more formal minster in Canterbury itself, which is probably when the Roman ruins were first substantially reoccupied. Augustine had been sent by Pope Gregory and represented the Roman church. In a letter of 598 to the patriarch of Alexandria, Gregory had boasted of the early successes of the Christian mission that he had despatched 'to the end of the world'. He followed this up in 601 by sending instructions to Augustine on how to organise things in England as he mistakenly believed that a Roman urban administrative framework had survived there.

Instead Augustine had found a fragmented, rural, post-Roman society in which to operate. The surviving Romano-British church, now thought of as the Celtic church, had not disappeared but had retreated from the paganism of the south-east and continued in Celtic north and west Britain and Wales. After nearly 200 years Celtic liturgies had not surprisingly diverged from those of Rome. In 603 the first meeting took place between St Augustine and leaders of the Celtic church. This was arranged by King Æthelbert I of Kent via the Hwicce, the Romano-British people of the area around Gloucester and Bath, who had successfully acculturated with both the West Saxons to the south and Angles to the east and north whilst retaining some of their cultural identity and church organisation. Bede writes that the meeting was at 'St

Augustine's Oak', on the border between the Hwicce and West Saxons, perhaps near Wychwood in Oxfordshire. A second meeting followed at Abberley in Worcestershire probably close to the border between the Hwicce and Pengwern, another area to the north of the Hwicce. It was attended by seven bishops of the Celtic church, who were singularly unimpressed by Augustine and the meeting ended with no agreement of co-operation or unity being reached.

Æthelbert I's prestige may have dropped after this ecumenical failure and Kent started to have a slow but unstoppable decline in importance and influence – although it still retained links with the Franks of northern France. After Æthelbert I's death there were a succession of short tenure Kentish kings, but even so Kent held on to some influence over Surrey.

Egbert became King of Kent in about 664. He established an abbey at Chertsey in Surrey, which he must therefore have still held. Egbert died suddenly in 673–675, which led to a crisis as neither of his sons was of age and the Mercians under King Wulfhere promptly took Surrey from Kent, then Kent itself was invaded and occupied by the Mercians.

In 675 the Meonwara of south Hampshire and the Wihtwara of the Isle of Wight, both of the same Jutish extraction as the Cantwara of Kent who had been subsumed by Mercia, were 'added' to Sussex by Mercia, as part of a 'deal' to ally Sussex and Mercia after sub-king Æthelwalh of Sussex's baptism. This appears all to have been part of Wulfhere's policy of pressuring the neighbouring West Saxons from both the north and the east. Eighteen months later the Cantwara rallied behind Egbert of Kent's younger brother Hlothere. Kent was retaken and later Hlothere got as far as controlling London (OE Lundenwic), the first Kentish king to do so since 616. He also probably regained Surrey. Later he agreed to share power with his nephew, Eadric, who became sub-king of West Kent (Kent, west of the Medway). Eadric, not liking that King Hlothere held the rest of Kent as well as being his overlord then made an unusual alliance with the South Saxons.

Kent and Sussex had avoided conflict, possibly since the time of Ælle, maybe because of the buffer zone afforded by Hæstingas and the fragmentation of Sussex. Eadric now encouraged the South Saxons to attack Kent, and one interpretation suggests that he possibly used as an inducement to do so the offer of control of the somewhat disputed Hæstingas. This would have meant the South Saxons crossing into east Kent via Hæstingas, presumably without much opposition. Hlothere was killed in the ensuing battles. So in late 685 Eadric got his wish and became King of all Kent, possibly having de facto ceded the sub-region of Hæstingas to the South Saxons, or at least acknowledged that Hæstingas was nominally part of Sussex.

Overall, there continued to be huge political, dynastic and military manoeuvrings in the major kingdoms of England before 900. During this period the South Saxons appeared to be allied to Mercia, while Kent was more aligned to the West Saxons.

This situation placed Sussex in an uncomfortable position. So, the South Saxon move described above appears part of the larger disturbance. But Kent had had about two centuries of near stability with only a small 673–675 hiccough. A reasonably accurate list of the Kings of Kent is given below.

The position of Sussex continued to be difficult. Cædwalla, a West Saxon who had been exiled, mustered an army and invaded Sussex from the west before 685. His initial success was short lived as he was beaten back by Sussex's Ealdormen Berhðun and Andhun. He regrouped and gained full control of Wessex by 685 and was back in Sussex by 686, killing the ealdormen and King Æthelwalh. Within two years he had taken control of all Surrey, Sussex and Kent. He swept through and fully annexed Sussex, presumably again crossing the hapless Hæstingas territory (although this is not specifically recorded) into Kent which became a battleground between Mercia and the West Saxons, with Kent finally occupied by Cædwalla. In 686–87 he left Mul, his brother, to rule Kent in his name.

In 687 the Cantwara revolted and Mul, with twelve of his companions, was trapped and burned to death inside a house. Cædwalla responded vigorously by laying waste to Kent, but seemingly with little effect on control. In any case he soon had to abdicate as he was dying from a wound previously received in fighting the Wihtwara (the Jutish 'cousins' of Kent) in and around the Isle of Wight in 686. *ASC(A,E)* records him as going on pilgrimage to Rome in 688 and dying there. His West Saxon successor, Ine, withdrew from Kent, but kept hold of Sussex, ruling it through sub-kings (see below).

687 saw Mercia pounce on Kent. The Cantwara, only just recovering from Cadwalla's rampage, were unable to resist and Kent became a Mercian vassal kingdom. Sighere of Essex, a client king of the Mercians, may have then governed Kent for a short period (687–88), before King Æthelred of Mercia appointed Oswine, who was probably descended from the Kentish King Æthelred, as sub-ruler of Kent. This was in the mistaken belief that the Cantwara would accept him as king because he was 'one of their own'. He may have clung on as sub-king up to 690, after which he was succeeded by Wihtred, the youngest son of the former Kentish King Egbert. Details are somewhat unclear as there was a co-ruler, Swæfheard of Essex, also placed by Mercia who survived Oswine by two or three years and may have also briefly co-ruled with Wihtred, but eventually Wihtred entirely freed Kent. In 694 Wihtred settled with Ine of the West Saxons over the killing of Mul, giving Wessex £30,000 [(*ASC A,B,F*) – the value or weirgeld of a royal heir's life] – and the two kings agreed on the borders of Kent, Surrey and Sussex which confirmed the Kentish loss of Surrey, and may have settled the issue of the Hæstingas territory. After this the West Saxons and Kent were between them able to keep Mercia at bay until the time of King Offa.

692–717 saw Sussex have one of its more identifiable 'sub-kings', Noðelm also known as Nunna, who granted land to his sister Noðgyð and others in four charters.

He was styled 'Nothelmus rex Suthsax' in the body of one charter, but he signed it as Nunna rex Sussax'). Noðgyð was granted land to build a minster, and in the charter it states that she promised to be 'Bishop Wilfrid's nun' and to go on a pilgrimage. Noðelm's last surviving charter, in which he was called 'Nunna rex Suthsax', is dated 714, probably in error for 717, so his reign began in or before 692 and ended in or after 717 (*Sawyer references S42–45. See below for more details of these charters*).

725 started with the death of Wihtred of Kent. He bequeathed Kent to his three sons, Alric, Æthelbert II and Eadberht with each son taking his own district to govern. Alric quickly 'disappeared' but his brothers appeared to rule harmoniously. Æthelbert II initially governed east Kent and Eadberht west Kent. Later Eadberht was also regent of east Kent from 747, when Æthelbert II became a recluse. Eadberht soon appointed a new sub-king to manage west Kent, firstly his own son to about 762, then Eanmund who may have become King of all Kent in 762–764. The situation concerning Æthelbert II and Eadberht *et al.* is confusing as Bede's *Historia ecclesiastica gentis Anglorum* ends here – and with it goes much of the detail of Kent's history. After this, charters remain the major source of information (*see Sawyer S1–41*). A reasonably accurate list of the Kings of Kent is given below in tabular form

Mercia turned on Kent again in 764 when Offa of Mercia moved into Kent. Offa made a sudden personal visit to Canterbury and manoeuvred his own candidates Heaberht and Egbert onto the Kentish throne in order to keep out the West Saxons. Any transitional rulers of Kent disappeared. Offa's imposed rulers came from Kentish noble lines, probably descended via the Oisingas female line from Oisc, the founder of the Kentish dynasty in 448. However Offa was unable to prevent the election of Jænberht, a former abbot of St Augustine's, and his opponent, as Archbishop of Canterbury.

Despite this, Mercian power was in the ascendant. Sometime in 770 Offa had gone on to subjugate Sussex but equally clearly the Hæstingas were somehow not initially included in this, which would suggest that Mercia had first entered Sussex from the west and/or north. This would be rectified one year later – in 771 the chronicler Simeon of Durham recorded the defeat of the people of Hastings (L *gens Hestingorum*), Hestingorum is the genitive, meaning 'of Hæstingas') by Offa of Mercia. It is not clear if this was done via Kent or Sussex or was a pincer movement from both. The action has the appearances of a 'mopping up' operation as Hæstingas had been left as the meagre content of a Mercian sandwich between Sussex and Kent. A charter of Offa records the foundation of a minster (a mother church serving a parochia from which developed several later parishes) at Bexhill in 772. Offa's grant was of eight hides of land to enable Bishop Oswald to found a minster, with the land reverting to the bishopric of Selsey (later Chichester) on Oswald's death.

Offa signed himself 'King of all the English' on two charters of 774–775 which were intended to trap Jænberht, Archbishop of Canterbury, into accepting the Mercian king's over-lordship. No reference was made at this time to any sub-king of Kent, and the ploy met with unexpected resistance when Egbert (Ecgberht) II backed by the Cantwara suddenly assumed control of all of Kent, with some help from the West Saxons. So, after a decade of subjugation Kent rebelled against Mercia. Egbert was able to defend Kent, beating Mercia at the first Battle of Otford (776) and ruling for about nine years, possibly with support from Cynewulf of the West Saxons. Egbert died sometime between 779–784 and his son Ealhmund succeeded him.

In 779 Offa had defeated Cynewulf of the West Saxons at Bensington (Benson in south Oxfordshire). But it took another five years for Offa to return his attentions to Kent. In 785/786 Ealhmund was killed and Offa moved in again. From this point forwards Kent would only three times briefly reassert any independence (796, 802 and 823) and remained most of the time until 825 under the control of Mercia. In 790 Offa and then in 795 his duke Beorhtwald on his behalf granted lands at Pevensey, Hastings and Rotherfield to the Abbey of Saint Denis in Paris. In both cases the word Hæstingas is used in the original Latin of the charters.

Sussex after 770 would never be an independent kingdom again and would stay under the thrall of Mercia until in about 823, when for a brief two years a person called Baldred managed to take power in Kent. By 825 he may have also been in control of Surrey and Sussex (if so crossing Hæstingas…?). This was a very short lived supremacy as when Ecgberht of Wessex defeated the Mercians at the Battle of Ellandon in 825 the sub-kingdoms of Essex, Sussex and Surrey also submitted to him. The West Saxons then rapidly moved into Kent, presumably in a pincer movement through both Sussex and Surrey led by Ecgberht's son, Æthelwulf, who saw off Baldred and therefore seized the whole of the south-east for Wessex. With respect to Ecgberht, the Cantwara may have been content to have him as king as he was descended from the Oiscingas Kentish kings via the female line.

Wessex took control and Surrey, Sussex and Kent were ruled by Æthelwulf, based in Kent as a sub-king. Sussex had become a province of Wessex. After 839 following Æthelwulf's accession to the throne of Wessex, the presumptive heir of Wessex remained sub-king in charge of Kent, Sussex and Surrey – and also from now onwards kings were to have Kentish, not West Saxon names. In 857 Æthelwulf confirmed the holding by the Abbey of Saint Denis in Paris of lands at Rotherfield, Hastings, and Pevensey in Sussex; and also in London (*Sawyer S 318*). Again, the name Hæstingas is used in the original untranslated Latin charter.

In 860 when Æthelbert became King of Wessex, the positions of sub-kings of Sussex, Surrey and Kent were abandoned, and they became full provinces of Wessex.

Danes. The blights on the horizon were Danish attacks which had started to threaten Kent from very late in the eighth century. From the mid-830s these increased in frequency. There was a large raid into the Romney area in 843 and in 870 the Danes attacked Wessex, whose forces were now commanded by King Æthelred and his younger brother Alfred. At the battle of Ashdown in 871 Alfred routed the Viking army, but after this Wessex suffered some defeats. His brother died and in 871 Alfred, to be the Great, became King of Wessex. Alfred was a man of letters and the arts (figure 38) and is known to have held estates in the Hæstingas area around Beckley/Ewhurst and also around Rotherfield.

In early 878 Danes led by King Guthrum landed via Poole harbour and rowing up the River Frome seized Chippenham in Wiltshire. They used it as a base from which to raid heavily and start to occupy Wessex. The West Saxons were reduced to guerrilla warfare. But in May 878 Alfred's army defeated the Danes at the Battle of Edington, following which Alfred concluded peace with them with the Treaty of Wedmore. Many of the Danes went to East Anglia where they joined Danes that had already settled and in 886, Alfred negotiated a partition treaty with the Danes, to form an area known as 'The Danelaw' where Danish customs and law pertained. Alfred had retained control of western and southern Wessex including Sussex, regained control of Kent, but also gained west Mercia. This was to be the future kernel of England.

The Danish threat remained, and Alfred restructured the Wessex defences. Firstly, he reorganised his army, and secondly was the architect of a defensive series of Burghal Hidage forts or fortified towns, with local examples (figure 39) near *eorþe burnan** (which literally translates as 'Earth Stream' and is probably Castle Toll near Newenden) and at *hæſtinʒa ceaſtre** (the original Hastings, Hæstingaceastre). If Castle Toll is Eorþe Burnan this burgh took the form of an 8 Ha (20 acre) enclosure on a low peninsula which was defended primarily by the marshland of the then River Limen on three sides and by a broad bank and ditch on the southern side. Partial excavation of the southern ditch in 1971 showed that it was not completed in its intended form and was reduced in scale and remained unfinished. There is a strong possibility that this is the unfinished Eorþe Burnan of the Burghal Hidage, mentioned in the *ASC* for 892 as having been 'an incomplete fort' attacked by the Danes, whose fleet of 250 ships made landfall at Appledore in Kent and sailed up the river.

Alfred also had built a navy of new fast larger ships giving him a defence in depth against Danish raiders. Alfred died in 899, aged 50, and was buried in Winchester.

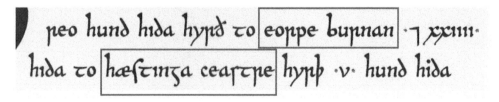

Figure 39. Excerpt from the Burghal Hidage transcription by M Butler after Nowell (BL- Add MS 43703 255r), concerning Eorpe Burnan and Hæstinga Ceastre.
OE Spellings from Nowell's transcription via Butler's copy.

Hæstingas is mentioned in the *ASC* for the last time in 1011 in conjunction with more huge Viking raids involving Sussex and Hæstingas. But Hæstingaceastre as a place name survived perhaps another 200 years, certainly beyond 1066 as its name is embroidered on the Bayeux Tapestry HESTENGA CEASTRA, with a second example of HESTENGA, as shown in figure 40.

Figure 40. Excerpt from the Bayeux tapestry

So, what are the conclusions of the quite detailed discussion above? Maybe before the term Hæstingas was coined it is unlikely but not impossible for a battle to have taken place at Penhurst/Ashburnham between South Saxons and Romano-British and/or Jutes from Kent. We can infer that the name Hæstingas was applied to this small but distinctive part of present-day East Sussex and its people for maybe 600 years, certainly from before 701 (possibly from *c.* 500) until at least the late 11th century.

Sussex itself was seldom a unitary kingdom and often under the over-lordship of others, or briefly crossed in transit e.g. in 683/5 and 823/5; but the person 'Hasten' or 'Hæsten' who gave rise to the name Hæsten ingas – people of Hæsten – is unknown.

If an estimate is made that the western boundary of Hæstingas was either from the inland north-west point of the Pevensey levels extending into the Weald towards Heathfield (which would virtually correspond with the western boundary of the Norman Rape of Hastings), or more modestly along the line of Wallers Haven from the north-east boundary of the levels, and in both cases the eastern boundary was the River Limen we can make an estimate from Domesday of how many people lived in the area pre-1086: 5,000 to 6,000. Also, if the area of productive land to support 'hæſtinȝa ceaſtṛe' in the Burghal Hidage is correct the total area covered by this might also correspond to the part the Norman Rape of Hastings south of the Wealden Forest.

Clearly seafaring, maybe some early ship building, and fishing would have developed at Hæstingaceastre (from its small ports at Bulverhythe [OE Burg wara hyð] and the Priory valley), at Rye (OE Atter ie, L Ria, Rya) and Old Winchelsea (OE Wincel-ea) where a fishing village may have been established on a shingle bank across Rye Bay in about 800. Salt panning was carried out on the Rye/Rother Camber and around Pevensey and early farming would have been carried out on the better land including on Alfred's estates at Beckley (OE Beccan-lea) and Rotherfield (OE Hryðeranfelda), as well as at all the -hams, -ings, -inghams and ingtuns, -felds and –leahs.

Most of the time Hæstingas appears to have been ignored by neighbouring Sussex and Kent, although it probably had more cultural connections with Kent than has been thought in the past if we take into account the place name, field structure and Frankish influences that have been described.

Hæstingas was of course going to have a sudden severe shock in 1066.

Rulers of Sussex and Kent from 491(477) until 900

Notes on all the tables below:

At the start of this period Sussex (Suð Seaxe) appears to have been a far from a unitary kingdom and seldom in total control of its own affairs. In the tables below yellow shading represents full control of the Kingdom of Sussex in its own right, starting with Ælle who invaded 477 but who could not be said to be in full control of until 491. He may or may not have been succeeded by one of his sons, Cissa. There follows a blank period, with no information, when it is assumed that Sussex was fragmented, and data is uncertain.

By 686 Sussex was subjugated by Wessex, but this broke down in 722 in a somewhat confused way with tenuous information. There appears to have been a struggle against Wessex and a split of Sussex into East and West, with the possibility of some linkage of part of Sussex to Kent in the East – no doubt involving the Hæstingas. The sub-king Watt may have also been something to do with Hæstingas, but this is tenuous. Once this period was over Sussex became subjugated by Mercia, until an upstart, Baldred, briefly moved into Kent, only to be removed rapidly by Æthelwulf, son of Ecgberht of Wessex after the Battle of Ellandon in 825. Æthelwulf became sub-king of Kent, plus Surrey and Sussex – a position the heirs presumptive of Wessex held until the position was abolished in 860 and Wessex was ruled as a unitary kingdom. The key to the colour shading of both tables below is:

	Sussex independent, with periods of being a client kingdom
	Uncertainty
	Mercian supremacy
	Kent independent, with periods of being a client kingdom
	Wessex Supremacy

No claim of absolute accuracy is made for the tables. They are best efforts to bring together data from sometimes conflicting sources.

Table 1: Rulers of Sussex from 491 (477) until 900

Year			
(477) 491	Ælle		
515?	Cissa		
No mention until about			
661	Wulthere of Mercia appoints and allies Athelwalh to 685		
	Sub-King	Ecgwald	
		Ealdormen: Berthum (d.686) Andhun	Wihtwara and Meonwara ceded to Sussex
	Cædwalla (685–688)	Sussex subjugated by Wessex	
	Ine (689–726)		
	Sub-Kings of Sussex Noðelm (692-717) Watt (?in East) (692-700) ?Osric (700-?) Ealdorman Bryni (c700-?) Sub-King Æthelstan (714-722)		
722	Possible revolt against Ine of Wessex led by Ealdbert		
725	Æthelbert may have continued the struggle vs. Wessex in the West.		
	Possibility that Eastern Sussex may have recognised Æthelbert II of East Kent		
758	Uncertain – possibly dual kingship West: Osmund East: Ealdwulf		
770	Offa of Mercia subjugates Sussex	Hæstingas subjugated 771	
	Sub-Kings: Oswald (772–?)Oslac (?776–785)Ealdwulf (?-791)		
791	Direct Mercian rule		
	Ecgfrith		
796	Cœnwulf		
821	Ceolwulf I		
823	Baldred	Seized Kent (+Sussex) from Mercia. May have been an opportunist Mercian	
825	Ecgberht of Wessex (802–) defeated the Mercians at the Battle of Ellandon. Kent, Surrey and Sussex became part of Wessex, with Sub-King of Sussex, Surrey and Kent his son Æthelwulf		
839	Æthelwulf	Sub-King of Sussex, Surrey and Kent Athelstan to 851 then Æthelbald	
858	Æthelbald	Sub-King of Sussex, Surrey and Kent Athelstan to 851 then Æthelbald	
860	Æthelbert	Position of Sub-Kings abolished	
865	Æthelred		
871	Alfred		
899	Edward		

Names, relationships, spellings and dates in Kent can all be very confusing, particularly at first. Multiple sources have been consulted, and these often conflict and confuse issues further, so there is again a repeated disclaimer to say that the table below is a best effort with no guarantee of absolute accuracy. The situation is made more difficult by the frequent adoption of dual kingships in Kent and supremacy changes with appointments of sub-kings.

about 447	Horsa (d.450) and Hengist	Foundation myth first rulers. Nicknames.	
488	Oisc/Escus/ Æsc	Name uncertain, may be generic	Founder of Kent Dynasty 'Oiscingas'
512	Octa/Ossa	?Son of Oisc. Controls Surrey and Middlesex	There is considerable name and date confusion at and before this point. There may have been more kings as Ossa and Octa may be different people.
540	Eormenric/Hermenric	Also assumed control of Essex	
560	Æthelbert I	Defeated by Ceawin of Wessex, Wessex pushes Kent back to East Surrey. Still overlord of Essex	First Christian king of all Anglo-Saxon kingdoms
616	Eadbald	Loses over-lordship of Essex	
640	Earconbert		
664	Ecgbert I	Still has control over parts of Surrey	
674/5	Hlothere/Lothaire	Later controls London and possibly Surrey Sub-King of West Kent/Surrey is Eadric, son of Ecgbert.	In about 683 Eadric gets South Saxons to invade East Kent and following several battles Hlothere is killed in 685
685	Eadric		Cædwalla of Wessex invades Kent

686	Cædwalla	Mul Sub-king to brother Cædwalla of Wessex	Mul killed and Caedwalla's successor Ine withdraws from Kent but holds Sussex
687 688	Æthelred I	Sighere/? Sæberht Mercian client king of Essex	Cantwara revolt. Mercia invades Wessex.
690		Oswine (–690) Sub-king of Kent, co-ruled with Swaefheard of Essex who for 2 more years may have co-ruled with Wihtræd	Oswine a Mercian placeman but of 'Oisingas' decent. Wihtræd a son of Ecgbert I (664) above.
About 693	Wihtræd	Brother of Eadric. Frees Kent. Bequeaths Kent to 3 sons	
725	Æthelbert II (East Kent)	Eadberht I (West Kent)	Alric (dies)
747	Eadbert I (all Kent)	Sub-King of West Kent Eadbert II	
759		Sub-King of West Kent Eanmund	
762	Eanmund/Sigured		
764	Offa	Subjugated by Mercia	
764 c.770		764–764 Sub-King Heabert From c. 770 Sub-King Ecgbert II	
773/774	Ecgbert II	1st Battle of Otford 776 at which Kent defeats Mercia	Declares Kent independence
779/784	Ealhmund		
785 787	Offa Son Ecgfrith co-ruled from 787	Mercia retakes direct rule	Both Offa and Ecgfrith died in 796
796	Eadbert II Praen	Rebellion without church support	Origin uncertain, said to be 'a priest'
798 807	Cœnwulf	Sub-King Cuthred Ealdorman Oswulf	Mercia mercilessly retakes Kent
		Ealdorman Eadwald?	
821	Ceolwulf II		
823	Baldred	Seized Kent (and Sussex) from Mercia. May have been an opportunist Mercian Ealdorman	

825	Ecgberht of Wessex (802–) defeated the Mercians at the Battle of Ellandon. Kent, Surrey and Sussex become part of Wessex.	Sub-King of Sussex, Surrey and Kent was his son Æthelwulf
839	Æthelwulf	Sub-King of Sussex, Surrey and Kent Athelstan to 851 then Æthelbald
851		
858	Æthelbald	Sub-King of Sussex, Surrey and Kent Æthelbert
860	Æthelbert	Position of Sub-Kings abolished
865	Æthelred	
871	Alfred	
899	Edward	

Table 3: Sawyer – List of Charters of kings and sub-kings of Sussex, and after that of King Offa of Mercia, Æthelwulf of Wessex and Edgar of England

For Sussex these are S42–S49 (*E-Sawyer references*). This is a sparse record of only eight charters, only one fifth of the numbers of records for Kent (S1–41)

They are followed by four curious documents (S1186, S133, S318 and S686) involving Hastings and Pevensey and supposed *Charters to the Abbey of Saint Denis of Paris*. These attract attention as various authorities have doubted their origin and suggest they are spurious, with some caveats that they may be based on genuine originals. The question is why would Offa or his duke, Beorhtwald, wish to grant valuable land and salterns to an abbey in Paris? A possible answer is in the table below.

Osmund (of Sussex) ?758 or ?765–?772 (2)
S 48. 762 probably for 765. Osmund (king), to Walhhere, his comes (count); grant , of 12 hides (tributarii) at Ferring, Sussex. For the construction of a minster at Selsey
S 49. 770. Osmund, king, to Wærbald, comes, and his wife Tidburh, for St Peter's Church (Henfield); grant of 15 hides (manentes) at Henfield, Sussex, with later confirmation by Offa, king of Mercia.
Æthelbert (of Sussex) ?733-? (2)
S 46. 733 x (747 x c. 765). Æthelbert, king of Sussex, to Diosza; grant, for the construction of a minster, of 18 hides (tributarii) at Wittering, Sussex, with a note of the transfer of the land by Diosza to his sister and confirmation by Offa, king of Mercia
S 47. Æthelberht, king of Sussex, to Wilfrid, bishop; grant of a half-hide (tributarius) at Chichester, Sussex.
Noðelm/Nothhelm/Nunna (of Sussex) ?692-?714 (4)

S 45. 692. Nothhelm (Nunna), king of Sussex, to Nothgyth, his sister; grant, in order to found a minster, of 33 hides (cassati) at Lidsey, Aldingbourne, Lenstedegate (? Westergate in Aldington) and (North) Mundham, Sussex. , Selsey
S 44. (a) c. 705 x (? 716 x ?). Nunna, king of Sussex, to Berhfrith, famulus Dei; grant of four hides (tributarii) at Peppering by the river Arun (Tarente), Sussex. , Selsey
S 43. 775 for c. 705 x c. 717. Nunna, king of Sussex, to Eadberht, bishop; grant of 20 hides (tributarii) at Hugabeorgum and Dene (probably East and West Dean near Chichester, Sussex), Selsey
S 42. 714 (? for 717 or 724). Nunna, king of Sussex, to Beadufrith and the brethren of Selsey; grant of 4 hides (manentes) at Herotunun, 3 (cassati) at Tættæshamstede and 3 at Sidlesham, Sussex, Selsey
S 42. 714 (? for 717 or 724). Nunna, king of Sussex, to Beadufrith and the brethren of Selsey; grant of 4 hides (manentes) at Herotunun, 3 (cassati) at Tættæshamstede and 3 at Sidlesham, Sussex, Selsey

After the subjugation of Sussex

S1186. 795. Berhtwald, dux, to the Abbey of Saint Denis; grant of land at Rotherfield, Hastings and Pevensey. Berthold was a 'sub-regulus' with some devolved powers of grant. ... (use of) my possession of the harbours, which are in the same area, beside the sea, Hastings and Pævenisel, together with saltpans and all that belongs to them. This grant is dubious but if true seems to have been in thanks for a miraculous cure after visiting Saint Denis. He also built a church at Rotherfield for the same reason. The church at Rotherfield is still called St Denys, a relatively unusual dedication in England. This gives some credence to the story.
S133. 790 (Tamworth, Staffs., 12 April). Offa, king of Mercia, to the Abbey of Saint Denis; grant of privileges for land at London, and confirmation of land at Rotherfield, Hastings and Pevensey, Sussex. Confirmation of S1186.
S318. (London, Nov.). Æthelwulf, king of the English, to the Abbey of Saint-Denis (Paris); confirmation of land at Rotherfield, Hastings and Pevensey, Sussex and in London .... And in Pevensey also salterns....
S686. 960. King Edgar to the Abbey of Saint-Denis, Paris ... restoring to the abbey animals (300 sheep and 50 cattle), salt production and farms which had been appropriated by the reeve Togred from the estates at Rotherfield, Hastings and Pevensey.

6
The Re-Christianisation of Eastern Sussex

Wilfred ... taking his way into the province of the South Saxons,
which extends from Kent to the south and west, as far as the
West Saxons, containing land of 7,000 families, and was at that
time still in bondage to pagan rites, he administered to them the
Word of faith, and the Baptism of salvation.

King Ethelwalch* gave to the most reverend prelate, Wilfrid,
land to the extent of 87 families, to maintain his company who
were wandering in exile. The place is called Selaeseu,** that is,
the Island of the Sea-Calf; it is encompassed by the sea on all
sides, except the west, where is an entrance about the cast of a
sling in width.

Bede's *Ecclesiastical History of England* (681 AD)

ollowing the Anglo-Saxon invasions, paganism, never far from the surface in Sussex, re-emerged in south-east England, although Christianity clung on in Britain further north and west. It is possible that Hæstingas then stayed pagan until the early eighth century when Christianity started to redevelop from Kent and western Sussex.

Once King Offa of Mercia had taken over Hæstingas he appears to have encouraged new churches to aid conversions. Maybe he regarded the area as a missionary zone as he provided the assets to support a new minster church at Bexhill in 772. Although

---

*   Ethelwalch = Æthelwealh who was ruler of the South Saxon kingdom from 661 until his death in 685. He was baptized in Mercia on marrying Princess Eafe, who was the daughter of Eanfrith, the king of the Christian Hwicce. He was the first Christian king of Sussex.

**   Selaeseu = Selsey

by no means certain, at the same time he may have encouraged the building of an church of St Helen at Ore in Hastings, a minster at Peasmarsh and maybe a church at Udimore and others, including yet another minster at or near Pevensey. Certainly, by the time of the Conquest the Hastings area was well churched, although little or nothing remains of these as the churches would have been mostly wooden structures.

In pre-Conquest times the Benedictine abbey of Fécamp had influence within the extensive manor of Rameslie from 1017. After that they probably established churches at Old Winchelsea, and at the township which they are presumed to have started or took over at Rye, and certainly the original two churches in what is now Hastings Old Town, which area was at the time within their manor of Rameslie. An unconfirmed charter of Fécamp Abbey suggests that they were also given a pre-existing church at Burhna (Eastbourne) by King Edward the Confessor in 1054.

Anglo-Saxon Minster Churches in Eastern Sussex

There can be little doubt that the 'planting' of one, probably two, or even three, minster churches in the eight century, to act as nuclei for other Anglo-Saxon churches around them, was a large step in the Christianisation of eastern Sussex, which had significantly lagged behind Kent. These small monasteries, to be known as minsters, were worldly institutions whose priests were known as 'clerks' or 'canons' who were in modern parlance developing 'outreach' into their local hamlets and villages. In 1086 clerks are sometimes mentioned by name in Domesday Book, holding small parcels of land pre-1066 off which they will have lived and received rentals. At other times, in *Domesday Book*, a church is mentioned in the areas covered by the minsters or within the lands of Fécamp abbey e.g. at Guestling. Overall the recording of churches and priests in Domesday Book is very erratic.

Peasmarsh

With respect to Peasmarsh, it is known that the post-Conquest prebend of Canon Theobald of Hastings College of Saint Mary in the Castle (a prebend was an allowance which was usually obtained from specific sources, in this case a share of each nominated parish's income) was later known as the prebend of Peasmarsh, because the lands of a former Peasmarsh minster made up the bulk of the endowments – which included the lands belonging to four other churches at Iden, Beckley, Northiam, and Playden.

The Peasmarsh minster is recorded as having been built on the same site as the Norman church which replaced it after 1070. The Bexhill minster is better recorded than that at Peasmarsh which is 'inferred', although Gardiner makes a very persuasive argument concerning its existence. It may have been related to the fact that there was a large royal manor around Beckley, probably including the other villages mentioned above, which is mentioned in Alfred the Great's will.

Bexhill

Much more is known about Bexhill. King Offa in the charter *S108*, dated 772, but probably updated around 1000, provided the assets to support a new minster church to bishop Oswald (Osa) of Selsey. This charter has sometimes been regarded as dubious and we only have a later copy of this which may have been somewhat altered when transcribed in the 13th century. A translated version, with words modified to correct the order of subjects, verbs, and objects, has been provided by Porter. This shows some interesting details of the location of the eight hides (or 'cassati') of land (in modern terms a total of up to about 1000 acres or 400Ha [=4 square kilometres], so not insignificant) provided in Bexhill as well as assets in other nearby locations to provide financial support. The location is interesting as the charter reads:

> These are eight hides relating to the inland of the land of the Bexware* first to the servants tree, from the servants tree eastwards and up to the old marsh dyke, then south to the treacherous place, along the beach (strand) over against Cooden (Coden) cliff, north to Kayworth or Kewhurst (Kæia weorð) and to the bending stream, north through Shortwood to the landmark beacon, from the beacon to the haunted ford, from the ford along the water to the street bridge, from the bridge up along the drainage ditch to the bedan pool, from the pool along the boundary thus to the servants tree.... *Bæxwarena land i.e. the land of the people of Bexhill

Translated onto a map this locates the land as being a large parcel north of the Cooden cliffs, not at all the location of Saint Peter's church in Bexhill old town, which was the nucleus of old Bexhill and sited further east. Faith discusses this in her *The English Peasantry and the Growth of Lordship* and she has produced a small sketch map corresponding to the above deduction. The land description is also wrong for an old church at Northeye, where later there was a flint chapel dedicated to St James, and in any case its date of dedication was way too late. The other supporting lands were located as follows:

> gavel-land appurtenant to Bexhill, namely, Barnhorn, Worsham, on Ibbanhyrste (?), Crowhurst, on Hricge (Ridge), on Gyllingan, Foxham (somewhere in Crowhurst), on Blacanbrocan (? Black Brooks near Westfield), and Icklesham, all in Sussex.

Domesday notes two churches at Bexhill, but only one definite site is known, which is the present St Peter's church. The Saxon features at Saint Peter's (some stonework uncovered in 1878, in the form of flint-rubble laid in herringbone courses) and the finding there of an intricately carved slab of local fine grained sandstone (figure 41) do not however exclude the possibility that it may have been the second church, not the minster. Faith concurs with this conjecture. The slab (pictured below) may even have been moved from the minster to St Peter's if and when it demised. Clearly we have no other potential archaeological location of the minster or any other church at this time (apart from 'somewhere' within the four sq.km). So the minster may indeed have been on the site of Saint Peter's and the large piece of land reported above may have only been used for its financial support and food production.

It is also noted that the Bishop of Chichester before the Conquest held two pieces of land in Bexhill, one of 20 hides (fitting the four sq. km) the other of only half a hide. The smaller one is of a size to accommodate a church and a house for the bishop.

Similar arrangements to those of Peasmarsh may have also once applied to a second canon's prebend at Hastings Collegiate Church, which took over the Bexhill minster 'parishes'. These included pre-Conquest churches in Hooe, Ninfield, Bulverhythe, Bullington (near Worsham/Pebsham) and Bexhill. Because of these linkages it has been presumed that small Anglo-Saxon churches (probably wooden) had been created in these locations pre-Conquest and that these and the minsters were further developed or replaced by early Norman stone churches in the early post-Conquest period.

Figure 41. The Saxon grave slab from St Peter's church
From http://www.stpetersbexhill.org.uk/history.html

…and around Pevensey too?

Gardiner has proposed that the later parish of Pevensey fell within the extensive territory of the minster at Bexhill, so there is some confusion. There had been ecclesiastical holdings (salterns and tenements) at Pevensey held by firstly Saint Denis and later Fécamp abbeys pre-Domesday and the Bishop of Selsey (later Chichester) had burgesses providing income within the borough at Domesday. Also no fewer than three priests, Edmer, Ordmer and Doda, were mentioned at Pevensey in Domesday, receiving rentals from 15, five and three burgesses respectively – considerably more than anywhere else in eastern Sussex, so it is very likely that there was a pre-Conquest church of some kind at Pevensey. One of the priests there, Eadmer looks as if he also held Herstmonceux, and another, Doda, one further west but the circumstances of these are undiscoverable. It is likely that they contributed to the upkeep of a minster at Pevensey. *Domesday Book* records another place called Horsey, not the islet called Horse Eye, at nearby Eastbourne Hundred. At Horsey after the Conquest one hide was held of 'Saint Martin's Church' by a clerk of Fécamp called Roger, but this church name does not correspond to the names of the later churches of either Pevensey or Eastbourne.

The Anglo-Saxon Churches of Eastern Sussex

Eastern Sussex appears to have been well churched in late Anglo-Saxon times (figure 42). Many of the churches seen today were recreations on the same sites in stone, post-Conquest – but it is extremely rare to find any Anglo-Saxon component as all have

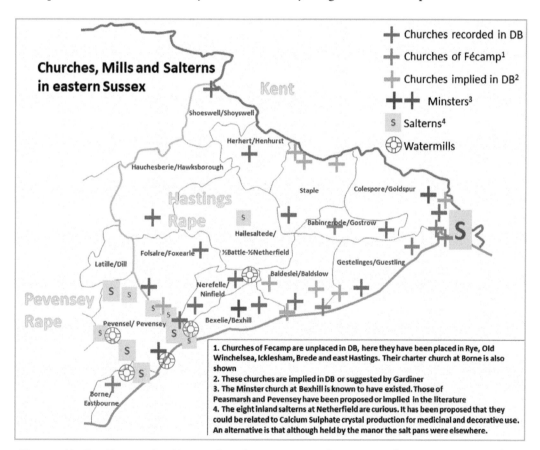

Figure 42. Pre-Domesday Saxon churches in eastern Sussex. For later convenience this map also shows Hundred boundaries and the salterns and mills mentioned in the area in Domesday.

Domesday data for this map is in the Appendix. Map © Keith Foord been rebuilt, some several times. In later times those at Old Winchelsea were washed into the sea. Those at Rye and Hastings were burnt by the French.

Plus those of Fécamp?

It is almost inconceivable that the Abbey of Fécamp would not have incorporated an early, possibly wooden, church at Rye in their 'new' borough, created as a trading centre. Also if required those probably dedicated to St Thomas and St Giles, at Old Winchelsea and also the original churches, now represented by the later buildings, on different sites, of All Saints and St Clement on its land at Hastings.

We cannot know the dates of first foundation of these churches, if they even existed, as no records exist. But Fécamp owned the Rameslie manor, which was most of Guestling hundred plus Brede. Abbot John of Fécamp is known to have visited England in 1054, and all these sites were within 'Rameslie' from well before the Conquest. It would be highly unlikely that they would not have provided the inhabitants of their various settlements with at least a small church.

And surely there would have been a church, possibly a minster church from well before the Normans arrived, at or near Pevensey, which Taylor postulates was within the roman walls at Pevensey. As noted above the Bishop of Selsey, Æthelric II, was receiving rentals from burgesses there and the priests seen in Domesday may have been based there, to minister to the people of the hundred and those working at Fécamp's saltpan holdings, and maybe also provide a priest for Fécamp's church at Bourne (Eastbourne). Might one or the other have been called Saint Michael's church (see Appendix)?

After the Conquest Bishop Æthelric II was deposed in 1070 and replaced by Bishop Stigand (not to be confused with Archbishop Stigand of Canterbury), who moved the see to Chichester, and the 'monks of Mortain' had replaced the TRE priests by 1086, probably well before that.

7

Organisation, early Settlement Names and Land Ownership in eastern Sussex before 1066

In most regions and localities there is a distinct pattern (to villages and towns) in their siting and their distribution, which is closely related to topographic features, drainage and soil conditions.

Trevor Wilde

The origin of the name Rape as a county division in Sussex is something of a mystery, although an early North Germanic precursor has been proposed as the word 'hreppr' in Old Norse can mean 'a share or an estate held in absolute ownership'. An alternative is OE 'rap', meaning rope – in this case perhaps used as a method of measurement.

They were not something imposed by the Normans, since Domesday sometimes implies that they or something like them existed 'tempore regis Edwardi' (in the time of King Edward [TRE]), i.e. before 1066. See for example, **9,122** and **9,125** (*in the Appendix: the figures in* **bold** *here and later are Phillimore* **Sussex** *DB references, unless prefixed otherwise*). But the Normans did modify them. The Rapes of the county that William the Conqueror evolved for Sussex after 1066 were part of William's post-Conquest early strategic defensive moves, to protect specific coastlines and land borders, and there were similar areas elsewhere in England – except that no others were called 'Rapes'.

Pre-1066 English precursors to the Rapes manifestly existed by the early tenth century, although they may not have been called Rapes, and the names and boundaries were not always the same. They possibly paralleled the Lathes of Kent, although the latter appear older and were well-defined areas pre-Conquest (it may be of course that they were just better recorded). These larger groupings of hundreds into district divisions might have been called by the peoples of eastern Sussex 'Lathes', for Lathe, not Rape, courts persisted in both Pevensey and Hastings Rapes post-Conquest, for some hundreds of years, which indicates a possible persisting Kentish influence. As always in eastern Sussex (it seems to the author) pre-1066 concepts are historically vaguer than in Kent and therefore become historically more controversial.

The system may have had some roots in the Burghal forts system of King Alfred, within which there were areas of supporting hidage to each fort, which for Hæstingaceastre was meant to be about 500 hides, and for Eorpeburnan 324 hides. It is difficult to compare that with the available hidage TRE as the way in which hidage was assessed may have been different pre-900 to the way it was counted on the eve of conquest. The size of the hide could vary within the county, and in relation to a land's productivity meaning that hides in land with low fertility could be physically bigger than those where there was good land. Additionally, some hides were not taxable. There were specific reasons for these variations, but in each district the reasons could differ.

This burghal system in turn may have had even earlier roots, via the earlier 'Tribal Hidage' in which 7th century Sussex consisted of 7,000 'hides' which were divided fairly equally between eastern and western Sussex as divided by the River Adur, which runs north-south. Later TRE, there were about 1,600 hides to East Sussex, presumably each of about twice the size of those of the Tribal Hidage. Sometimes they became grouped into hundreds, but there was a great variation of total hidage between hundreds. Locally the hundreds had OE names TRE, often relating to a significant settlement, but others have names like Babinrerode and Hailesaltede, names which seem to defeat students of onomastics.

To complicate matters for those trying to interpret these issues it has been noted that some of the imposed Norman Rape boundaries cut through the middle of hundreds, and hundred boundaries cut through villages. One-third of the town of Lewes lay in Pevensey Rape, but the other two-thirds of Lewes and the South Malling manors were held as tenant-in-chief by the Archbishop of Canterbury. The names, borders, and numbers of the internal divisions of Sussex were repeatedly adjusted, although Hastings Rape appears to have been relatively unaffected by this medieval gerrymandering. *Domesday Book* tersely reports only on how they were at one instant in time in 1086, with echoes to the time of King Edward the Confessor and maybe before that.

The absence of an entry for Hastings within the Baldslow Hundred of the Rape of Hastings in *Domesday Book* has caused some consternation to historians for centuries. This was, however, not a unique situation. There are several similar blank spaces at the start of other counties' entries in *Domesday Book*, and blank spaces for Winchester and London. Where these 'spaces' contain entries, such as for Dover in Kent, the first entry is always a borough. It has been conjectured that in virtually every county there were boroughs, requiring different treatment to the standard *Domesday Book* recording. These were either never finally recorded or were too big for the space left for them, or they were recorded separately, and the recordings have been lost.

There is however a *Domesday Book* recording of a 'new', but obviously small, Hastings just inside the adjacent Hundred of Guestling within the manor of Rameslie. This may be our first hint that all was not well with 'old' Hastings or Haestingceastre – and that a 'new' Hastings was developing slightly to its east in the shelter of the small Bourne valley.

It is now considered that the original Hastings or Hæstingaceastre or Hastingaport lay on a hill to the west, between the Priory Valley, now the main commercial centre of Hastings, and Bulverhythe. This would have been in the different Hundred of Baldslow. Places in this Hundred, now subsumed into Hastings and St Leonards, are named in *Domesday Book*, such as Filsham, Hollington, 'Cortesly' and Bulverhythe. It should be noted that Filsham was a very large manor with 15 hides (1800acres/730ha) of productive land and was formerly held directly by King Edward himself. Post Conquest, about half this manor was directly held by the count of Eu and the rest held from him by 11 others. Filsham would appear to have supported over 100 households, and there were another 70+ families in adjacent manors, which might suggest a population of nearly 1000 in the area of the presumed Hæstingaceastre.

Domesday Book has the additional information that, post-Conquest, 20 burgesses are recorded paying rent for three virgates (90 acres/36ha) of land directly held by the Count of Eu at Bollington, which was in the area of Pebsham/Worsham, on the western side of Bulverhythe. By then most of the rest of Bollington belonged to the Norman Abbey of Tréport. Were these the displaced town burgesses of Hæstingaceastre, now paying rents for nearby land, as their former holdings had been wrecked in 1066?

Bexhill/Bollington between them had a recorded population of about 150 families: say nearly 700 people; Ninfield plus Hooe had about 100 households, say 500 people. The site of the Battle town-to-be was in the adjacent Hundred of Hailesaltede (later split into the half-Hundreds of Battle and Netherfield) with no recorded population at that location pre-1066, but there were a few households in the area of present day Battle, at Penhurst (2) Netherfield (6), Uckham (4), Mountfield (11), Whatlington (9), Catsfield (13) and Ashburnham (24).

So, taking into account other nearby small manors and some undercounting by *Domesday Book* agents the whole population of the Hastings/Bexhill/Battle area alone at that time may have about 2,000.

Rye appears to have been of some size, with 64 burgesses (as long as it actually was the new borough of Rameslie, which seems a reasonable conclusion). It is impossible to know how big the borough was or exactly when it was founded before 1066, but the suggestion is that it had been developed as a trading centre by the abbey of Fécamp after the acquisition of Rameslie, and they called the settlement variously 'Rie' and 'Ria' in their cartulary. One source has suggested an earlier Anglo-Saxon settlement, but this cannot be fully corroborated. There had been some Roman activity nearby at Playden.

Old Winchelsea, if it was founded in about 800 as some believe, may have been of moderate size for the time, but was more likely to have been a small fishing village until later coastal changes allowed its port to develop after the Conquest, when its importance and population grew. Some have hypothesised a much earlier foundation of Winchelsea as a seat of a sub-kingdom of Sussex related to a grandson of Ælle called Wine Cissa, but this is purely conjectural.

The pre-1066 population of the three most eastern hundreds may have been about 1,500.

We know that there was some Roman settlement around Eastbourne and Pevensey, but what about later? At Pevensey evidence of a small Saxon settlement of the 6th–7th century has been found but after this it appears to have had only sparse settlement until about 950. The township lay at the end of the small peninsula and there was little land for food growing in its immediate vicinity. There were a few nearby small satellite manors, but its hinterland away from the marshland has some good land. It was certainly used as a centre for salt-making with some tenements which are mentioned in early charters. As its port developed it seems to have rapidly grown post-950 so that it had 52 burgesses before 1066, making it of a similar size and wealth to post-Conquest Rye. According to the cartulary of Fécamp Abbey, in December 1054 Edward the Confessor gave to that abbey a church at Burhna (Eastbourne) with supporting land at Horsey and Lantport (?Langley) and more land, some salterns and twelve tenements at 'Caestra' (by which must be meant around or inside the walls of Pevensey castle). But it is curious that their ownership of these TRE is not directly mentioned in *Domesday Book*. By 1086 Pevensey was called a borough and had a mint – but there is no record of a pre-Conquest mint. Over 50% of these burgesses paid rentals to the church, probably split between Fécamp Abbey and the Bishop of Selsey, with the rest paying the king.

The surrounding Hundred of Pevensey was moderately large, not surprisingly as it was mostly water, extending eastwards to Hooe Levels, and northwards to the adjacent small Hundred of Dill beyond Hailsham. Both these areas included extensive ploughlands and hidages, but of course they included all the embayment including all the small isles or eyes, marshlands and salt-producing areas, so its population appeared sparse compared to areas further west in the Rape of Pevensey. Hailsham was only a small place with just four recorded households. These two hundreds, including the borough of Pevensey may have accommodated just under 700 souls. In the Hundred of Eastbourne the total recorded number of households in scattered developments is 71, possibly 97, representing a population of about 350–500.

In the immediate pre-Conquest years, King Edward or his sister Countess Goda held a good number of manors around Hastings, including a large one at Filsham where Edward was lord of 15 hides, within which the Hastings burgh may have been sited, if it was not in the adjacent Cortesley manor which has disappeared with little trace, probably eroded away into the sea.

Goda held a total of 142 hides in small estates aroundRngland, but there were definite clusters of estates in her hands in the northern part of the Rape of Hastings and rather more in the eastern part of the Rape of Pevensey. In eastern Sussex she must have held 25–30 hides in all. King Edward may have given these lands to his sister soon after his accession, but she could have received them later after her second marriage, to Count Eustace II of Boulogne, was annulled in 1049 almost certainly for political reasons. She had married him in 1035 after the death of her first husband Drogo of Mantes whom she had married in 1024. Bates has postulated that the handing of these east Sussex estates to Goda may have been to block their acquisition by the Godwins, although there is no proof of that.

Godwin family lands in eastern Sussex included estates at Ninfield, Crowhurst, Whatlington and Udimore. It has been noted that the Godwin family overall held more English manors and estates than the king at this time. Contrary to general opinion, in eastern Sussex whilst they held several important estates, their holdings were outnumbered by royal estates held by King Edward or his sister Countess Goda and there were also prominent church estates. Sussex is normally quoted as 'being a Godwin stronghold' and across all Sussex they did indeed hold 40 vills valued at a total of £880 – averaging to a substantial £22 per vill. In eastern Sussex the figures are 13 and £34, more like £3 per vill, but one third of their numerical holdings – and of much less value!

The hundreds of Foxearle and Ninfield held areas of good farmland as well as salterns and supported a large population of around 1250. A slight surprise is the additional estimated population of around another 1250 for the three northernmost Hundreds of Hastings Rape, Hawksborough, Henhurst and Shoyswell, which have often been considered as thinly populated. Many settlements in these three Hundreds were actually attached to Pevensey estates. These are closely clustered and marked 'P' on figure 43 below, which shows the pre-1066 lords of vills, Hundred boundaries and the estimated population in the Hundreds of eastern Sussex at the end of Edward the Confessor's reign. The ownership data is taken from the TRE data in *Domesday Book*, which is collated in tabular form in the Appendix.

Sussex was part of Wessex, of which in the years before 1066 the earls were Godwin Wulfnothson, appointed by King Cnut in 1020 as Earl of all Wessex, followed on his death in 1053 by his son Harold Godwinson. From the information in the Appendix and other sources, it is clear that their holdings were rather more prominent in central and western Sussex than in the very east, where royal holdings (by King Edward or his sister Countess Goda) in value terms are about double those of the Godwins.

The ecclesiastical holdings in eastern Sussex are also significant. We do know that Harold Godwinson had tried to wrest Rameslie from the Abbey of Fécamp and now we can see why.

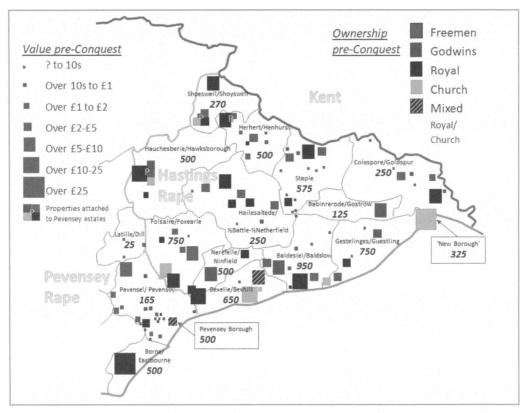

Figure 43. Pre-1066 values and holders of manors, hundred boundaries and the estimated population in the hundreds of eastern Sussex at the end of Edward the Confessor's reign. See appendix for more detail

The pre and post Conquest names of hundreds are given. Population estimates after Brandon ©BDHS

It can also be noted that the church, royal and Godwin holdings were normally larger and/or much more valuable than those of 'lesser' mortals. But some of these 'lesser' mortals held much more land, sometimes in multiple counties, than others who basically held only solitary small-holdings. This did not make them invulnerable to loss of their lands post-Conquest. Everything, with some ecclesiastical exceptions, initially went into the hands of William. A few of the larger English landowners who survived the Battle of Hastings were granted post-Conquest some small portions of their TRE holdings. Thanks to the Hull group, we know of a few probably identifiable examples, both of those who survived and those who probably died in eastern Sussex at the Battle of Hastings. All suffered considerable reductions in or complete loss of their holdings and status. The numbers in brackets after their names represent their 'Prosopography of Anglo-Saxon England' (PASE) numeration to differentiate from others of the same name, here and in the appendix. The Phillimore references of their holdings are also given below for easy identification in the Appendix.

Young Alnoth (4), or Æthelnoth of Kent, was a major TRE landholder in 1066, with very large holdings totalling 341 hides in Buckinghamshire, Kent, Sussex, Surrey, Hampshire and Oxfordshire. In DB he is nearly always given the title cilt (young) and was known outside Kent as 'the Kentishman'. He was taken to Normandy amongst William's hostages when William returned in triumph to Normandy in 1067. He lost most of his holdings and lordships to Odo, Bishop of Bayeux. In eastern Sussex he lost Wartling (**9,6**) to William, Count of Eu and Hailsham (**10,68**) to be held by a man called William with the 11 salterns there being retained in lordship by the Count of Mortain. His huge 50 hide manor of Alciston (**8,1**) with four hides extra from Totnore hundred (**8,2**) were both given to Battle Abbey. In *OpenDomesday* he is recorded as holding on to a single property in Hampshire within the Lands of the Priory of Christchurch at Twynham, who were the tenants in chief (**Hampshire 17,2**).

Osw[e]ard (12), (**9,3 and 9,114**) probably Osweard of Norton, the TRE sheriff of western Kent was displaced by Odo, Bishop of Bayeux, half-brother of William the Conqueror, from his Kent and Essex estates. TRE Osward may have held two concentrations of estates, one group across Kent, Sussex and Surrey, the other in western England, totalling 133 hides. This covered 28 estates. He appears to have held on to a couple of virgates in Sussex at Filsham (part of Hastings **9,14**), and a further couple of quite small estates (**12,24** and **12,27**) near Portslade just west of Brighton.

Northmann (1) (**9,8 9.32, 9,86**) in spite of his name, which is an English construct meaning a 'man from the north', was not of 'Danish' origin and was a magnate in eastern Kent. All his holdings in Kent, Surrey and Sussex were held directly from King Edward. His total holdings were 88 hides. He appears to have been allowed to survive on a fragment of a small part of the manor of Frankwell in Ashburnham that he had previously held (**9,8**), serving as one of six men-at-arms for the Count d'Eu. The unusual name may mean that he was related to the brother of Earl Leofric of Mercia of the same name who was executed early in the reign of King Cnut (in about 1017).

Azur is a name of 'Danish' descent. An Azur or Azor was one of the wealthiest thanes in southern England. According to PASE a man *Azur (2)* 'son of Thorth' held 26 properties in Sussex totalling over 160 hides. His properties spread to Surrey and Wiltshire, with another cluster in the south Midlands. In eastern Sussex he only held **9,87**. Even this tiny holding was lost to Reinbert, Eu's new sheriff. PASE identifies him as one of King Edward's housecarls and he had probably witnessed royal diplomas in the 1040s. Most of his estates had been held directly from King Edward with a few from Earls Godwine and Harold Godwinson. There is some difficulty with the name as *PASE* identifies 37 Azurs or Azors. But 'the son of Thorth' otherwise know as 'Azur of Sussex' was by a long way the largest landholder. He may have survived Hastings as an Azur 'son of Thorth' still held one property in Berkshire in 1086.

An 'Azur' witnessed a gift of land by William the Conqueror for Wells Cathedral at Whitsuntide 1068. This may have been another Azur as a known man of that name was a bursar to King Edward and is also known to still be holding a little land in 1086. William had moved quickly after December 1067 when he had returned to England from Normandy (landing at Winchelsea) to transfer lands from the old English aristocracy to favoured Normans and the signature of an English thane or royal bureaucrat would have given a slight gloss of legitimacy to the deed. We hear no more of any Azurs after that.

Wulfmaer (31) was the priest at Filsham TRE **9,14** but also held 6 hides at Fairlight **(9,107)** and also probably held other lands further west in Sussex including **9,46** at Willingdon, from both King Edward and Earl Godwine, some of which were quite valuable. He is not heard of post-1066. The name is found in many other counties in *OpenDomesday* and *PASE*, but they cannot have all been of the same man.

Goda (16) **(9,22** and **9,23)** not to be confused with Countess Goda (*Goda 6 in PASE*), as well as holding a big estate at Folkington held further lands in Cambridgeshire and Suffolk, interestingly sometimes holding them from Northmann (above), with whom he must have been associated. He disappears after 1066.

Wulfbeald (1) **(8,3** and **9,25)** of Uckham and Beech (within the future large estate of Battle Abbey) and of Guestling (an enclave in the manor of Rameslie) is another man associated with Northmann elsewhere. He held four properties in Suffolk, two of which he held from Northmann. Wulfbeald disappears after 1066.

Cana (1) **(9,3 9,83 9,85)** held ten properties all over Sussex and four hides in Surrey at Tandridge (which is also mentioned below). These were all held directly from King Edward, which cannot be a coincidence, perhaps he was a royal servant of some kind. No post-Conquest record of Cana can be found.

Ælfhere (28) is of interest. An Ælfhere of Mercia was involved in Æthelred II's ascent to the throne of England. But being of elevated rank did not imply safety in those days. The family gradually fell down the power ranks and by the time of Cnut held only hereditary residuals of their former lands. The Ælfhere here, who may have been related, is the man holding the largish Ewhurst and Bodiam manors **9.12** TRE. He also held four more vills further west in Sussex. Men called Ælfhere who are probably not the same men held 14 more manors scattered across Gloucestershire and southern England, and with a biggish focus in Norfolk. In one entry he is noted as 'thane'. The Sussex properties all went to the lords of the Rapes in Sussex, and there is no further record.

Some of those who disappear probably fell at the Battle of Hastings or became completely dispossessed. Alnoth/Æthelnoth, Osweard and Northmann somehow survived and clung on to vestiges of their previous estates. They were part of

the flotsam and jetsam of an aristocracy wrecked in the storm of the Conquest.

Osweard had three small-holdings one with seven acres, a share of a mill, and some woodland for pigs, valued at £2, which he held of William of Warenne, lord of the Rape of Lewes. Alnoth was basically 'left out to grass' in moderate comfort on a small estate in Hampshire, and Northmann was reduced to a half a hide holding at Frankwell, near Ashburnham, whilst being a man at arms serving the lord of the Rape of Hastings. All three appear to have been men of some rank TRE, and as they survived Hastings, or maybe had not been at Hastings, were treated better than others. The above are all men of some substance about whom we have some small fragmentary details. They still had something. Ordinary folk would have switched masters and hoped for the best.

Battle Abbey, We do not know exactly who had occupied the lands TRE which would later comprise the land for the approximately 18.5 square kilometres (about 7 square miles) one league radius, nearly circular, banlieu or leuga or lowey of Battle Abbey – apart from the half-hide at Uckham which was held by Wulfbeald from Earl Godwin. In 1070 William had requisitioned these lands for his gift to the Abbey from the Count of Eu, and the new fief holding Normans who had 'acquired' it. This created a new 'Rape within the Rape', under the control of the abbot, not Eu, but not free of royal command – but then neither were the Rapes. When the acquirers complained he said that it was 'for their love of him' and with no compensation. When they infringed the hunting and forestry rights of the new Rape William issued a stern writ to Eu, witnessed by Earl William de Warenne, Lord of Pevensey Rape and copied to Haimo (the sheriff of Kent) and Archbishop Lanfranc of Canterbury etc.

... do the same justice on the men of Count Robert that you would do upon those who had done this in my own demesne......do right for the monks as you would do for yourself. And if there are any that do not wish to obey you, send them to me and I shall do right upon them.....It is my wish that you should look after them (the monks) in my place....

None of the details of the TRE holder or ownership of these seized estates was recorded in Domesday, although in **8,3** to **8,16** some of the additional lands that the abbey held directly or from d'Eu are named.

An interesting conjecture has been made and repeated by several authors that the core of the banlieu might have been a manorial outlier from the valuable estate of Limpsfield in Surrey, just east of Oxted, called in *Domesday Book* the manor of Bramswelle. William had gifted Limpsfield along with Bramswelle to Battle Abbey as part of their founding endowment. Darby and Campbell remarked on the fact that 'no value was given to 'Bramswelle' in 1086 (**Surrey 11,1**) and that after this entry it disappears from the Surrey records'. However, in the *Custumals of Battle Abbey (Edward I and II)* it becomes clear that there had been a name shift to 'Brodehamme', then Brod[e]ham, which is now Broadham Green, just south of Oxted. This remained a Surrey possession of Battle Abbey, and was later rented to the Priory of Tandridge, for in 1535 the Prior of Tandridge, paid 12d (5p) rent to Battle. It was also mentioned in a deed of 1345 when one John Stockett granted to Sir Robert Stangrave and Dame Joan his wife land 'lying between their wood on one part and the Abbot of Battle's manor (Broadham) on the other'.

Hastings. Returning to Hastings let us review the information available about its possible location. It has been strongly argued that William's original prefabricated wooden castle at Hastings would have been somewhere further west towards Bulverhythe, rather than at the present site of the stone castle of Hastings on the West Hill. The Norman wooden castle could have been erected on the site of the old burghal enclosure, and that is what we may be seeing in the *Bayeux Tapestry*.

Burghal forts were established in the late ninth century as English defences against Viking raids, and were part of the Alfredian strategy to recover all of England from the Danes, with the coastal forts designed to deter further Viking raids. We cannot definitely say that a burghal fort was not on the site of the Norman stone castle on the West Hill that is still a prominent feature of the Hastings skyline, but there is no archaeological evidence for this, nor for its occupation in Anglo-Saxon times, although there is some evidence of very early human occupation.

It has been hypothesised that it is likely that the Hæstingaceastre Saxon burgh was a fortified township, akin to Wareham or Wallingford, and somewhere to the west of the present centre of Hastings. Some slightly later records have been found that support this and the subject has been explored in detail by Gardiner. He located a record of a charter for a parcel of land in the parish of St Michael which was west of the Priory valley, dated approximately 1280, granting land north of a road leading from Hastings 'market place' towards Battle, from which we can infer that the market place was also west of the Priory valley – the first mention of such a market at Hastings was in 900, i.e. well before the later move to the Bourne valley. There was also a place name Esthethe (East Hythe) in the Bourne valley, with properties on each side of the stream. This suggests that a name differential was being made between places in 'new' Hastings in the more eastern Bourne valley (East Hythe?) and those that had developed in the more western Priory valley adjacent to the even more western 'old'

Hastings/Hæstingaceastre.

So the important part of all the above post-1066 conjecture, as far as pre-1066 Hastings or Haestingceastre is concerned, is that the fortifications that William established were likely, but not certainly, to have been on top of or within the burghal fortifications of Hæstingaceastre, which may have used the cliffs as part of its protection and had probably contained a number of pre-cursor Saxon churches probably named as mentioned above.

We know that in 1086 other areas around Hastings such as Wilting and Crowhurst were still waste or recovering after the predations of 1066, also that the 'castellaria de Hastinges' – castelry of Hastings (its direct jurisdiction) was given to the Count of Eu in 1069. The castelry of Hastings must have been most of the Rape of Hastings, minus some defined holdings – for example the banlieu of Battle Abbey and the lands held by Fécamp and Tréport abbeys.

Also the castelry would soon include Bexhill Hundred as bishop Ælric (of Selsey [pre-cursor to Chichester]) held Bexhill both before and after 1066 until its 'gift', after which one 'Osbern' (that is Osbern FitzHugh who founded a Bodiam dynasty and was related to Robert d'Eu and distantly to William I) then held it from Eu. This land was eventually returned to the Bishop of Chichester by King Henry II in 1148.

Settlement Names. But what were eastern Sussex settlements called before 1066? It must be assumed that all the places mentioned in eastern Sussex which are in *Domesday Book* (*DB*) existed before 1066, in the 'Time of King Edward' (TRE). Place name studies give us some idea of the earliest available names for these settlements, with a focus on the names of towns (and some of their early parts such as Filsham, within present Hastings) and villages and hamlets within the Rape of Hastings and the easternmost hundreds of the Rape of Pevensey.

The work of Mawer and Stenton, Brandon, and Roberts is heavily leaned on and only name versions from *DB* or earlier charters, etc. are shown below, in date of first appearance order if there is more than one name. There would have been many later variations, and additional places, some now long forgotten, or surviving only in the names of woods or farms, but here we concentrate on recorded and locatable pre-1066 settlement places only. Settlement names which only appear after 1066 are not included.

Table 4: Pre-Conquest names of settlements in eastern Sussex

The order in the table is generally by location, from west to east, i.e. Eastbourne to Playden and Peasmarsh near Rye. The list does not include 'disappeared' names or names which only appear after 1066. Names recorded in *Domesday Book* are preceded by 'DB', but it should be recognised that *Domesday* scribes' mis-spelled some TRE place names, presumably having some difficulty understanding the English locals' pronunciations.

Eastbourne: *Burhna*, Burneham, Eastburneham, DB Borne. *The small settlement would have been named after its stream or bourne. Burhna is used in a cartulary of Fécamp Abbey in 1054/5 to identify the location of a church, which they were granted.*
Willingdon: DB Wilendone
Horsey: Horsea, Horselie. *A different place, but has the same history as Horse Eye (below), that is having been an islet within the previous Pevensey embayment*
Hailsham: Possibly Æg[e]lesham, DB Hamelesham. *Probably derived from Ægel's or Haegel's ham(m), a personal name*
Hellingly: Possibly Hyllinga leah
Pevensey: L Anderita, L Anderidos, Pevenisel, Penuisel, Pefenesea, Peuenesea, Pefenesæ plus more similar variations and finally in DB Pevenesel. *The first element is a personal name Pefen, 'ea' is OE. for 'stream'. The 'sel' version is said to be a diminutive. Pevensey is the only place in eastern Sussex with a known Latin (L) name.*
Horse Eye: Horsiges *gemæro*, and as Horsey above
Horns (nr. Hankham) : DB Orne
Hankham: Hanecan *hamme*, DB Henecham
Peelings (nr. Hankham) : Pydelingas, DB Palinges, also Pellinges
Langley: ? Lamtport, DB Langelie
Otham: Ottanham
Westham: West ham
Ticehurst: Ticcenes hyrst (*OE. Kid's wood*), Ticcenesfeld, DB Ticefelle, also Titeherste
Hazelhurst: Hæselersc, DB Halsesse
Henhurst: DB Henhurt
Salehurst: Sealh hyrst (OE. Willow wood) DB Salhert
Etchingham: possibly OE. Eccingham
Warbleton: DB Warborgetone
Brightling: Byrhtlingan, Byrhtelingas DB Brislinga
Dallington: Possibly Deallantun, DB Dalintone

Penhurst: Pena's hyrst or Pen(n)hyrst, DB Penehest

Ashburnham: Æscburnaham, DB Esseborne

Herstmonceux: DB Herst/Herste. *The monceux part was a much later post Conquest addition*

Wartling: Wyrtel's ing or Wyrtlingas DB Werlinges

Catsfield: DB Cedesfeld and Cedesfelle

Hooe: DB Hou

Ninfield: DB Nerewelle

Bexhill: Bexlea, Bixlea, Bæxwarena land, DB Bexelei. *From 'byxe leah' – box tree clearing*

Barnhorn: Berna hornan, Byrna hornan – *personal name 'Berna' plus 'horna' – corner of land*

Cooden: Coden

Pebsham: Pyppel's hamm

Worsham: Wyrtlesham, Wyrtle's hamm

Hastings: Hæstingas, Hæsten's ing, Haestingceastre, Hestingport, DB Hastinges

Bulverhythe: Burhwara hyð

Netherfield: Probably Næddran feld (*OE. Adder field*), DB Nedrefelle, also Nirefeld

Mountfield: Possibly OE. Muntefeld, DB Montifelle

Uckham: DB Bocheham

Whatlington: Hwætel's ing (*people's*) tun (*farm*), DB Watlingetone

Baldslow: Baldes leah, DB Baldeslei, Badeslie

Crowhurst: Croghyrste, DB Croherst, Crohurst

Wilting: DB Wiltington, Wiltinges

Hollington: DB Holintune, Horintone

Filsham: DB Pilesham, also Wileshā

Ore: DB Orne

Westfield: DB Westwelle

Lidham: Hlȳda's ham, DB Luet or Ivet?

Fairlight: Possibly *OE. Fær leage*, DB Ferlega

Guestling: Possibly Grystel's ing (*people*), DB G(h)estelinges. *Grystel is related to 'grisle', i.e. a tough piece of meat*

Icklesham: Ikelesham, Icoleshamme. *Probably from Icel's hamm*

Iden: DB Idene

Pett: Possibly *OE. Pytt* (as in pit or well) DB Ivet or Luet? *Uncertain and could be confused with Lidham*

Rye: Rygebeorg, Atter ie, (*both possible, OE*), Ria (*Ria and Rie are both used in the cartulary of Fécamp Abbey and would have been used by them after 1033*. In DB it is not named but is included un-named within Rameslie manor

Winchelsea: Hypothetically perhaps *Winesceseley, Gwent-chesel-ey, Wincel-ea or Winceleseg, OE*. It has also been conjectured that 'Wincel' may be a diminutive of the name Winece, and '*ea*' is OE. for 'water or stream' and '*ieg*' for island. Germanic language relatives of '*Wincel*' suggest an 'in the corner' sense or 'island at or with a recess' and coupled with 'ieg' which evolved in ME to 'ie' it could have meant 'island with/at a bay or inlet', which is what Old Winchelsea may have looked like from further inland. *There was also some confusion of the name Wencles on a coin, which raised the possibility of a never proven mint at Winchelsea, but this has since been associated with other places as well.* Like Rye, Old Winchelsea was incorporated within Rameslie in DB. There have been a lot of ideas, just like Rye!

Brede: *Bretda (OE. Dated before 1042)*. In DB it is not named but is probably grouped un-named under Rameslie manor

Udimore: Udan (Uda's) – *mere OE.* (lake) or *gemœru OE.* (boundary), DB Dodimere

Bodiam: Boda's *ham*, possibly Bodesham DB Bodehā

Ewhurst: Iw or Eow *hyrst* DB Werste

Northiam: DB Hiham

Sedlescombe: Sedi comb DB Salescome, Selescome

Footland: DB Fodilant

Beckley: Beccanlea (Becca's clearing). *No separate mention in DB when it was probably grouped into a manor, which included 'Glossams' and 'Heighton' which are both mentioned.*

Iden: DB Idene

Kitchenham: DB Checehā, Checeham

Northiam: DB Higham

Peasmarsh: Possibly Pisa or Peosa *mersc*

Playden: Plega's *den* (swine pasture), DB Pleidenā

8
Eastern Sussex from 899 until the death of Harthacnut in 1042

Cnut was very large grown and strong of power, a very handsome man, when exempted that his nose was thin, tall and somewhat crooked...'

Knytlinge Saga

Kings in this period numbered thirteen. In chronological order and with mini biographies they were:

Table 5: English Kings 899–January 1066

EDWARD (The Elder) 899–924   Succeeded his father Alfred the Great.
ATHELSTAN 924–939   Son of Edward the Elder, during his reign individual kingdoms were brought together to create a single and unified England.
EDMUND 939–946   Succeeded his half-bother Athelstan as king aged 18. Re-established control over northern England, which had fallen back under Danish influence following the death of Athelstan. He died after being stabbed aged just 25. His two sons, Eadwig and Edgar, were perhaps considered too young to become kings.
EADRED 946–955   The son of Edward the Elder by his third marriage to Eadgifu. Eadred succeeded his brother Edmund but died in his early 30s, unmarried and without an heir.
EADWIG 955–959   The eldest son of Edmund I, Eadwig was about 16 when crowned. Eadwig died when he was just 20. The circumstances of his death are not recorded.
EDGAR 959–975   The youngest son of Edmund I.

EDWARD THE MARTYR 975–978

Eldest son of Edgar, Edward was crowned king when aged just twelve. Edward's short reign ended when he was murdered by followers of Æthelred.

ÆTHELRED II THE 'UNRÆD' 978–1013

Æthelred was 'Unræd' which was OE for 'badly advised'. He became king aged about ten. He fled to Normandy with his second wife Queen Emma and their children in 1013 when Sweyn Forkbeard, King of the Danes invaded England.

SWEYN FORKBEARD 1013–1014

Sweyn was pronounced King of England on Christmas Day 1013 but died just 5 weeks later.

ÆTHELRED II THE 'UNRÆD' 1014–1016

Æthelred returned in early 1014 after Sweyn's death. The short remainder of Æthelred's reign was one of a constant conflict with Sweyn's son Cnut, who re-invaded. His son Edmund, by his first wife, was the main proponent for the English.

EDMUND II IRONSIDE 1016–1016

The son of Æthelred II, Edmund had led the resistance to Cnut's invasion since 1015. He eventually made a pact with Cnut to divide the kingdom between them and ruled Wessex. Edmund suspiciously died later that year, possibly assassinated. Ælthelred II's younger sons by Emma, his second wife, the Athelings Edward and Alfred returned to safety in Normandy.

CNUT THE GREAT 1016–1035

Cnut became king of all England following the death of Edmund II. In 1017, he married Emma of Normandy, the widow of Æthelred II and divided England into the four earldoms of East Anglia, Mercia, Northumbria and Wessex. He died after a longish unknown illness aged about 45.

HAROLD I 1035–1040

Also known as Harold Harefoot he was the (possibly) illegitimate son of Cnut's first queen. He claimed the English crown on the death of Cnut whilst his (possible) half-brother Harthacnut (by Queen Emma) was in Denmark protecting his Danish kingdom. The *ASC* attributes his death aged about 24 to divine judgement!

HARTHACANUT 1040–1042

The son of Cnut and Emma of Normandy, Harthacnut sailed to England with his mother. He invited his half-brother Edward, Emma's son from her first marriage to Æthelred II, back from exile in Normandy. Harthacnut also died aged just 24, having had a convulsion whilst drinking. He was the last Danish king to rule England.

There is unfortunately a considerable paucity of charter information concerning eastern Sussex during these years, and although some events can be found in the ASC they tend to be general ones involving Sussex in passing. This means that in the text below when something is known it gets a disproportionately large review, as it is a glimpse into a very opaque window.

There were no local abbots to consider at this time but the Abbeys of Fécamp and

Tréport in Normandy and Saint Denis, Paris all had or claimed some interests in local manors and estates.

By 900 Sussex was within Wessex and the push to reconquer all of England and to encompass the English–Danish peoples of the Danelaw was usually well away from eastern Sussex, although the ports must have been called on from time to time for ships. Alfred had gradually pushed back the Danes that had settled in northern and eastern England, so that between 884–954 rule in England was shared between Anglo-Saxon law and the Danelaw (with a dividing line NW to SE generally following the alignment of Watling Street – the great Roman road from London to Shrewsbury). Although Alfred had already been recognised as the King of all the English some Viking raids continued. There was one particularly large raid of 250 ships landed not far away from the eastern Sussex boundary – at Appledore, Kent in 892, and it took no fewer than four more English kings – Edward, Athelstan, Edmund and finally Eadred to remove the Viking threat, and fully restore English rule across the whole of England.

After 900 the very first bit of direct information about eastern Sussex we have is from 900 itself in no less than Alfred the Great's will. He gave to his blood kinsman (?cousin) Osferth the manors of Beckley and Rotherfield, each considerably larger than just the named places. He also gae him manors at Ditchling, Southampton, Leominster, Angmering and Feltham. Beckley would have included Peasmarsh, Ewhurst, etc. This may be indirectly relevant to the development of Rameslie to its south, a large estate stretching from the Priory Valley of Hastings to Rye and northwards from the coast to the River Brede.

Rameslie

Rameslie, a primary estate of eastern Sussex, was of strategic importance at the time of the Norman Conquest. Its provenance is also of considerable interest as it involves an unusually detailed historical detective story. It should be noted that there are various spellings of Rameslie in old documents (and recent ones for that matter, with even more neologistic variations). These include Rameslie, Rameslege, Ram(m)es(s)leagh, Hrammeslege, Ramsley, etc., and these spellings will also be used interchangeably in this document, as in original texts. But what about the early history of this large estate, before 1017?

A resumé of Rameslie after 1017 notes that Emma of Normandy persuaded King Æthelred II (the Unræd) to grant it to the Norman Abbey of Fécamp, a favourite abbey of Norman dukes. This was probably as part of Emma and Æthelred's marriage agreement in 1002, between her father, Duke Richard II of Normandy and Æthelred. Fécamp was Emma's father's religious foundation, so of great importance to him and his children. The grant would have made sense as a demonstration of a political alliance between England and Normandy. Emma would therefore have had a personal religious interest, and maybe some additional political motivation in trying to secure this strategic area for Normandy.

This gift was not fulfilled before Æthelred's death in 1016. Bates considers that the transfer was not made because Duke Richard II continued to allow Danish warriors to use Normandy as a base, contrary to the objectives of the deal. In addition, there were two 'minor' difficulties about this as the manor already belonged to the Oxfordshire Abbey of Eynsham, and Eynsham's patron was an Ealdorman of Wessex, probably closely related to Æthelred II, who would demand very significant compensation.

Emma dealt with the matter soon after Æthelred II's death, when she married King Cnut in 1017. Emma played an active role in the signing of royal grants and charters, and she may have taken steps to make sure that Rammesleagh was signed over to Fécamp. Emma signed the grants that Cnut made in 1017 by which Fécamp was given the estate at Rammesleagh with its landing place, 'as promised by Ælthelred'. As for Cnut, Bates comments that it also made a lot of sense to confirm the grant, because Duke Richard II was now looking after Emma's children by her first marriage and because it was therefore important to keep him onside.

Some of Hastings was included in the original grant of the manor which comprised virtually all of the Hundred of Guestling and extended westwards into the Hundred of Baldslow as far as the present-day Priory valley of Hastings. In or just after 1028 a further charter or charters confirmed by Harthacnut after his later accession and signed by Emma added another estate at Brede (OE Bredta) and the revenue from two thirds of the tithes of Old Winchelsea to Fécamp's holding. Overall, although this second charter appears to be one document, it contains two documents which additionally refer to a third. Haskins says that the cartulary of Fécamp 'is not free from forgeries' but there is no doubt that the present Saint George's Church in Brede was founded by Fécamp in 1180 and if they had not legitimately held the land this would not have been the case.

This link with Normandy was to last four centuries, with odd breaks during hostilities with France, when ownership temporarily resumed to the English crown. The link may also explain why the Normans were happy to choose Hastings as their 1066 base, after their probable first choice of the Isle of Wight or Solent area became less achievable after the invasion fleet's move from Dives to St Valéry sur Somme (*see Foord and Clephane-Cameron*). The Abbey of Fécamp probably undertook a major development of a new borough starting well before 1066 but reported in 1086. This was on the then semi-island of Rye (as concluded by the *Romney Marsh Research Trust's Rye Project*) – this was almost certainly the 'new' borough described within the rather confusing entry for Rameslie in *Domesday Book* of 1086.

But how was it that a quite large manor, with 100 saltpans, 20 hides of arable land, plus meadows and other assets including a 'landing place' was in the hands of

Eynsham Abbey before 1017? Not only that, but it was probable that even before Eynsham held it that it had been held by Abbess Wulfwyn of the Saxon nunnery at Wareham in Dorset from way before 982. This mystery needs some detective work to find possible explanations and theories:

A nunnery and a possible monastery may have been founded at Wareham, in about 672. A 'monasterium of holy virgins' is recorded in Asser's account of the Danish raids on the town of Wareham in 876, when the nuns were presumably dispersed – although the physical survival of the minster church there is generally accepted. Tradition has it that the nunnery was re-founded in 915 by Æthelflæd of Wessex, a daughter of King Alfred (also known as 'Lady of the Mercians').

There is a record that Wareham Abbey was the first brief burial place of King Edward the Martyr, murdered at Corfe Castle in 978, before his body was moved to Shaftesbury early in the next year. The abbey was apparently still in existence in 982 when the death of its Abbess Wulfwyn is incidentally recorded in the *foundation charter of Eynsham* (1005). Wulfwyn had left Rameslie in her will to her kinsman Æthelmær to help him found his monastery. Knowles and Hadcock give a tentative date for the Wareham nunnery's dissolution as about 997–8, if so it would appear that Rameslie was actually in the personal gift of Wulfwyn, whose death pre-dated this.

In those days heads of nunneries were nearly always drawn from noble families and thus we can presume with reasonable confidence that Wulfwyn was of such a family. But there were restrictions on how women could hold land. Women could inherit land, but often estates granted to them were 'entailed', that is the women might enjoy their profits from the estates for life, but on death the estates reverted to their male next of kin and re-joined the family stocks. Yorke says that such restrictions seem to have applied not only to women in secular life, but also to those who entered convents. It is highly likely that it is via this route that Abbess Wulfwyn of Wareham bequeathed Rameslie to her male kinsman Ealdorman Æthelmær 'the Fat' (son of Ealdorman Æthelweard 'the Historian' of the Western Provinces [the western half of Wessex – Wiltshire, Somerset, Dorset, Devon and Cornwall]) who was the founder of Eynsham Abbey.

Æthelweard 'the Historian' claimed descent from King Æthelred I of Wessex, brother of Alfred the Great (i.e. he would have been the great^{x3} nephew of Alfred), so it is entirely possible that, if they were both of noble descent, that Wulfwyn and Æthelmær were related and that he was her closest male relative. Æthelweard wrote a chronicle, dedicated to his cousin Mathilda who was the great-great granddaughter of King Alfred. Also, his sister may have been the Ælfgifu briefly married to King Eadwig and then divorced on the grounds of consanguinity. In this context Wulfwyn may also have been a descendant of Æthelwulf, father of both Æthelred I and Alfred.

That Wulfwyn was a kinswoman of Æthelmær is clearly stated in Æthelred II's foundation charter of Eynsham Abbey dated 1005 (although as ever there is no absolute proof that Abbess Wulfwyn was the same Wulfwyn, although the Abbess is the only Wulfwyn of note of 982 and before that according to Searle's *Onomasticon*. The abbreviated charter, which is also a confirmatory list of the abbey's supporting manors and estates reads:

> 1005. King Æthelred to Eynsham Abbey; confirmation of the foundation by Æthelmær, the endowment including ...... Rameslege with its harbour or landing place bequeathed to Eynsham by Wulfin (Wulfwyn), Æthelmær's kinswoman.

It is clear from numbers of studies that Æthelmær had been working for some considerable time pre-1005 to obtain the land (mainly by exchanges) plus sufficient income from other manors to support building a new abbey at Eynsham. For example, as early as 983, King Æthelred II himself granted land at Thames Ditton in Surrey to Æthelmær. In addition, he and his father Æthelweard were high in court circles, were each in turn Ealdorman of the Western Provinces (the son probably succeeding his father in about 1002) and signed numerous charters. Æthelmær had chosen Aelfric, with whom he had worked at Cerne Abbey, in Dorset (which he had re-established in 987), to be abbot of Eynsham. Æthelmær also planned to live his last years at this abbey. Monks had been recruited, buildings erected, boundaries clarified, endowments settled etc. The 1005 charter was the final seal of royal approval. So, referring back to Queen Emma's wish to obtain Rameslie for Fécamp Abbey, it was unlikely that Æthelred II would upset his trusted courtier's plans. In fact Æthelmær lived on until about 1013, at which time England was in turmoil and under sustained attack from the Danes led by King Sweyn of Denmark. Sweyn would seize control of all England in 1014 and his son King Cnut would do so more securely in 1016 after the deaths of Æthelred II and Edmund Ironside.

Æthelweard the son of Æthelmær also became Ealdorman of the Western Provinces in turn, but fell afoul of Cnut, who had him executed in 1017. The vacancy created was filled soon afterwards by Godwin Wulfnothson, father of Harold Godwinson, but that is another story. The other son of Æthelmær, Æthelnoth, fared somewhat better becoming Archbishop of Canterbury in 1020.

Cnut made an astute political move to secure the south coast of England from possible attacks from other Danes based in Normandy by 'setting aside' his first wife and marrying the widowed Emma, a princess of Normandy, moving the Dukes of Normandy 'onside'. After her marriage to Cnut in 1017 Emma moved quickly and the first part of Rameslie at last belonged to Fécamp, news of which may well have greatly pleased the Norman court. Brede was added to this estate well before 1066.

There is one final conundrum. How and when did Wulfwyn inherit or obtain the grant of Rameslie in the first place? The grant of such a large estate, not over heavily populated but with the income from its 100 salterns (it was one of the largest salt-making areas on the south coast) and other resources would suggest a noble donor. Looking at the pre-Conquest ownership of nearby manors we can note that many, perhaps more than usual, were held by an ealdorman of Wessex, the king or a near relative of the king. But a number of other valuable manors were held ecclesiastically.

There is also a possible local parallel estate: Playden and adjacent places are considered to have been part of the large Saxon estate north of the River Tillingham centred on an eighth century Saxon minster at Peasmarsh that included Playden, Iden, Beckley and Northiam. But it is noted in *Domesday* that before 1066 Northiam had Earl Godwine as its overlord and Playden's overlord was King Edward. Post-1066 the overlord became the Count of Eu. Neither Beckley nor Peasmarsh are mentioned in *Domesday* although some of their component parts are, but in Alfred the Great's will he granted the large 'manor of Beckley' to a kinsman. And Eorpeburnham in nearby Newenden was probably an incomplete Alfredian burghal fort.

'The manor of Beccanlea … and the lands that thereto belong'

was left to his kinsman Osferth, who was possibly Alfred's illegitimate son. Certainly he was closely related to the royal family as twice he is noted as having 'consanguineal kinship' to Alfred the Great and he is prominent in the lists of those signing charters during the lives of three kings – late in the life of Alfred, all of Edward the Elder's reign to the start of King Athelstan's. He signed at least 34 surviving charters; his last recorded signing being in 934. In *PASE* he is entered as 'Osfrith 8' although by far the most frequent spelling if his name is 'Osferð'. In Alfred's will the addition of the phrase '… and all the lands…' raises the possibility that the whole of the minster estate may have been held by Alfred pre-900 – might it also have extended to include Rameslie?

Nelson, who examines Osferth's closeness to the throne, goes as far as to query if the bequest to Osferth was in fact the core of a South Saxon sub-kingdom? This to the author of this book raises the spectre of 'Hæstingas', which may have been that sub-kingdom's name. Whatever the situation, the pre-1066 Anglo-Saxon beginnings of the above settlements are indicated by Alfred's will and the three *Domesday* entries, and all the place names are clearly of Old English origin.

Much as we may postulate about who owned what and exactly who was the donor of Rameslie to Wulfwyn the actual benefactor turns out to be impossible to determine. The available primary Saxon literature has been researched by many scholars, but the relative rarity of these sources means that sometimes only tenuous family links can be made between even high-ranking nobles – sometimes using, what may be called by some, 'flexible logic'. If we dared suggest possible donors of Rammesleagh to Wulfwyn the prime candidates appear to be Æthelflæd of Wessex and her royal nephews, or later Ealdorman Eadwine of Sussex who died in 982.

So, we know a bit more about Rammesleagh than many have supposed, via the above historical detective story, but much remains conjecture. What we can postulate, with no certainty whatsoever, is that is that if it was originally held by Alfred and was passed to Osferth who died sometime after 934, it may have then passed after Osferth's death directly to Wulfwyn. However, it probably ended up in the hands of an unknown person or persons (still possibly of royal or noble descent) – the last of which became, sometime before 982, the unknown donor to Wulfwyn. Wulfwyn then gifted it to Æthelmær in her will of 982. Later it was formally transferred to Eynsham Abbey before Queen Emma spotted her opportunity in 1017 to transfer it to another ecclesiastical body, but this time one in Normandy, the possible results of this being why this subject is of such interest here.

The initial Rameslie estate occupied the majority of Guestling Hundred, except for the enclaved manors at Guestling itself (held by the king pre-1066 and comprising 4½ hides [225ha]) and Lidham (held by one 'Godwin' pre-1066, comprising 1 hide [50ha]) and which together had a hidage of about 25% of the value of Rameslie's, although less value per hide. Later, Brede, in central Gostrow Hundred, was added. The Rameslie estate initially also included land within Baldslow Hundred (which corresponded to the 'Old Town', 'West Hill' and the eastern side of the 'Priory Valley' of present-day Hastings).

The Peasmarsh minster estate occupied most of Goldspur Hundred (less tiny Rye incursions) plus Northiam from the Staple Hundred. Post-Conquest the churches and glebe lands of its five parishes became the Prebend of one of the canons of the College of St Mary in the Castle at Hastings, consistent with some ecclesiastical continuity.

The other minster estate in the area, at Bexhill, had similar parishes at Hooe, Ninfield, Bullington, Bulverhythe and Bexhill and these parishes plus the parishes of All Saints, St Clement, St Andrew and Holy Trinity in Hastings which all later were transferred and constituted the Prebend of a second Canon at the College of St Mary.

There is no evidence that Udimore with its detached western parts was ever part of either estate. Immediately pre-Conquest Udimore was held by Harold Godwinson.

Not Rameslie … and Vikings

In 928, in King Athelstan's *Statute of Greatly* (made at Faversham), a mint was recorded as being at Hæstingaceastre. This must show that the town was a notable trading centre. Later Æthelred II was producing silver coins from 30 mints across the country, many to pay off the Vikings. The first surviving coins bearing the town's name date from 985–991.

There were five mint operators in Hastings in 1017–23, a later time of economic boom, but minting there was discontinued post-Conquest at the end of the reign of King Stephen (1135–54). One of the few surviving coins of King Harold Godwinson is held at Hastings Museum.

Although there continued to be sporadic Viking raids post-Alfred in south-eastern England, there had been nearly 100 years of relative peace until there were serious recurrences after 980. At first there were coastal raids mainly in Kent, but eastern Sussex would not have been spared some attention and by 994 the whole of the south coast from Essex to Hampshire was involved. A massive Viking attack on London led by Sweyn and Olaf Tryggvason occurred in 994, but they were beaten off and went off harrying, with the coast of Sussex one of their targets. In 997 a Viking army created a base on the Isle of Wight and after that their raids extended over the next 20 years with raids into Kent in 999. The biggest issue for the English was the ineffectiveness of Æthelred II the Unræd in dealing with them. Time after time he bought off the Vikings with Danegeld, which led to brief periods of calm, only for raiding to be resumed. The bribes to go away became bigger and bigger.

Vikings based in Normandy were also a problem and diplomatic approaches were made to Duke Richard I of Normandy to see if he would help subdue them, but by 990 feelings between Normandy and England became quite hostile. The Pope brokered an Anglo-Norman treaty in 991 but the Vikings still overwintered across the Channel.

The later event to try to help control raiding by Vikings from Normandy was of course the marriage in 1002 of Æthelred II to Emma, sister of the new duke of Normandy. The *ASC* (*E version*) for 1002 says

> And in the same spring, the Lady, Richard's daughter, came here to the land.

Emma took the Saxon name Ælfgifu for official occasions and to sign documents, which can be confusing as Æthelred's former wife was Ælfgifu of York and her future husband Cnut's concubine was Ælfgifu of Northampton. The marriage still failed to stop the Vikings using Normandy as a raiding base. It did, however, create some interesting general and dynastic issues which would come to haunt eastern Sussex and England as a whole

In 1009 a large Viking army landed in East Kent but were paid off with £3,000, after which they raided and burned extensively in Sussex, Hampshire and Berkshire, even though Æthelred had placed men throughout the coastal districts against their attacks. Then in 1011 the Vikings over-ran all Kent, Sussex, Surrey and 'Hæstingas' which appears to show that the Hastings area was still a significant and semi-independent locality.

In 1013 Sweyn of Denmark invaded with rather more serious intent. After briefly landing at Sandwich he sailed north to the Humber Estuary and landed his army at Gainsborough on the River Trent. All the threatened areas submitted, and he marched south. Briefly repulsed from London they went west, but soon returned, and London too capitulated. The growing difficulties meant that Emma fled for Normandy with her children later in 1013, and eventually Ælthelred was also forced to flee to join them, when:

> all the nation regarded him (Sweyn) as full king.

Sweyn had become King of England by conquest; however, he died suddenly just 5 weeks later. The Danes elected Sweyn's son, Cnut, king but in an about face:

> all the councillors of England, ecclesiastical and lay took council and determined that Ælthelred should be sent for, declaring that no lord was dearer to them than their natural lord 'if only he would govern them more justly than before.

Ælthelred came back, carefully first sending his son Edward to check things out, and then somewhat out of character rapidly attacked and drove off Cnut. Emma returned.

Cnut

In the summer of 1015 Cnut sailed back and proceeded to march through England.

> [Cnut] came into Sandwich and straightway sailed around Kent to Wessex, until he came to the mouth of the Frome, and harried in Dorset and Wiltshire and Somerset.

By the winter of 1015–16 Wessex had submitted and Cnut marched north-east through Warwickshire to eastern Mercia. Emma and her children were back in Normandy and Æthelred's oldest surviving son Edmund (Ironside) now took things into his own hands. Ælthelred II died on 23 April 1016 and this left a confused power vacuum with conflicts in many parts of England, but eventually Edmund after the second Battle of Otford somehow managed to drive the Vikings into Kent and on to the Isle of Sheppey. Finally, there was the evenly matched Battle of Ashingdon in Essex in October 1016 which Cnut just won, but afterwards a sort of brief co-ruling arrangement was made with Edmund in control of Wessex.

Edmund died suspiciously on 30 November 1016, and Cnut became king of all England. This was followed by high-level culling and numbers of high-ranking Englishmen were executed in 1017, including some relatives of Earl Godwin of Wessex.

Cnut had won a country that had a surprisingly stable government. He went on to weigh the pros and cons of making a political marriage. He was already married 'in the Danish way' to Ælfgifu of Northampton, whom he was prepared to 'put aside', and he arranged to marry formally Æthelred II's widow, Emma. So, a deal was done.

Cnut 'had her fetched' in 1017. Emma took an active role in the signing of royal grants and charters including those that signed over Rammesleagh or Rameslie to the Norman Abbey of Fécamp.

Cnut initially ruled Wessex himself, but placed earls in the other three English earldoms and sent his son Harthacnut as a child 'half-king' to rule Denmark with the assistance of a regent. Godwin Wulfnothson was appointed to be Earl of East Wessex (Hampshire, Berkshire, Surrey and Sussex, but not Kent) in 1018. After the Earl of West Wessex (probably Æthelweard) was outlawed, apparently for having caused some subversion whilst Cnut was away, Godwin took on the role of Earl of all Wessex from Cornwall to Sussex in 1020. It should be noted that Cnut was so clearly impressed by Godwin that he 'gave him' his brother-in-law Ulf's sister Gytha as a wife.

In or just after 1028, possible second charters, confirmed after his later accession by Harthacnut (*S982*) and also signed by Emma, added another estate at Brede (OE Bredta) and the revenue from two thirds of the tithes of Winchelsea to the Rameslie holding of Fécamp Abbey. Overall although there is one charter it appears to contain two documents which refer to three transactions.

Relations with Normandy started to deteriorate in about 1030. Duke Robert of Normandy may have married Cnut's sister Margaret/Esthrith Sweyn(or Svend)sdatter but had repudiated or divorced her. This is not recorded by Norman writers, who naturally tended to avoid writing about things that their dukes might not wish to be reminded of, but both Adam of Bremen, and Rodulfus Glaber (an 11th-century French historian) in his *Historiarum Libri Quinque*, both record (in a somewhat confused way) a marriage of a sister of Cnut (called Margaret or Estrith, probably the latter) to a duke of Normandy. If this happened Cnut would have been very displeased.

After Cnut

In England King Cnut's death in 1035 was somewhat unexpected. His oldest son Sweyn had been with his mother Ælfgifu in Norway acting as regent but being deposed had fled to Denmark where he died in 1034. So, he was out of the English succession issue. He was replaced in Norway by Magnus, son of Ólaf Haraldson. Cnut's son by Emma, Harthacnut, was still acting as regent in Denmark. Emma promptly manoeuvred on behalf of Harthacnut, but her stepson Harold Harefoot was in England. The Witan prevaricated and split over the succession, but Harefoot gradually gained ascendancy in England, except in Wessex where Harthacnut, through Emma as his regent and supported by earl Godwin of Wessex, was holding on. But Earl Godwin swung behind Harefoot and the Witan eventually made Harefoot 'protector' of all England in 1037. This made things very difficult for Emma and she fled to Flanders as Normandy was going through a period of instability.

If Harthacnut had promptly returned from Denmark he might have gained all

England for himself, but he was pinned down defending Denmark from Magnus, the new King of Norway. When the sitting Archbishop of Canterbury died in 1038 Kent was added to Godwin's earldom of Wessex, so that he now controlled all the south coast.

Early in this period, possibly encouraged by letters purported to be from Emma, but also suggested to have been a ruse by Harefoot, which may have implied that they had a chance of restoration, both Edward and his brother Alfred made almost simultaneous forays to England, which have been interpreted as attempts by them to regain the throne for the line of Wessex. Edward's attempt had considerable support from Normandy, but the expected English support was not forthcoming on his landing near Southampton and he retreated. Alfred's foray from Flanders was intercepted in Kent by Godwin's men. It was a disaster, some of his men were killed, others enslaved and Alfred himself had his eyes put out. Delivered to Ely Abbey he died from this terrible wound in 1036.

Harold Harefoot died suddenly at the age of 23 on 17 March 1040. The cause of death was some sort of illness, possibly suspicious, but the *ASC* pithily says it was 'divine judgement'. According to reports he certainly does not appear to have been a very nice person at all.

Negotiations between the English magnates and Harthacnut then dragged on a while, but eventually he and Emma sailed from Flanders just before mid-summer with a moderately large escort of 60 ships to Sandwich, receiving a good welcome. Harthacnut is said to have then had Harefoot's body exhumed and thrown into a ditch. It would seem that he had thoroughly disliked his half-brother. Harthacnut himself died on 8 June 1042. He just dropped down dead with a convulsion according to reports. He was drinking heavily at the time. He was only 24.

Harthacnut's reign was not popular, it seems something of a disaster, and in 1041 negotiations were held for Edward to join Emma and Harthacnut in government as co-ruler and heir presumptive. *ASC* (*C,D*) record loyalty oaths sworn to Edward in 1041). Godwin was involved as ever in this move. He had been promoted by Cnut and survived and had survived his sons. Now this ambitious true survivor and master of the realm would serve Edward.

9

Seventh Son, Exile, Contender, and Rightful Kings: Edward the Confessor, eastern Sussex and the origins of the Cinque Ports

A saintly, conscientious man of 40, much given to prayer and works of mercy, his early misfortunes taught him to deprecate all earthly ambitions, and he now concentrated fully on governing his people with Christian gentleness, justice and prudence.

Saint of The Day: 13th October

After Harthacnut's death in 1042, Edward, son of Æthelred II and Emma, was the only surviving son and heir presumptive of either Æthelred II or Cnut, but another Sweyn, Harthacnut's cousin by Cnut's sister Estrith Svendsdatter, also had a distant claim, and was also, it seems, the heir presumptive of Denmark, in spite of the above deal between Harthacnut and Magnus.

Much of the underlying detail related to this chapter is covered in *1066 and the Battle of Hastings – Preludes, Events and Postscripts*. Where there are new modification or additions to this, the details are expanded here, and modifications will be made to its next edition.

The focus now turns mainly to Edward and the Godwin family that served him and leans heavily on the recent biographies, *Edward the Confessor* by Licence and *William the Conqueror* by Bates for the most modern interpretations. Some lesser items of local interest are included of course, but the story inexorably leads to the main event that will happen in eastern Sussex in late 1066 after the death of Edward the Confessor.

Edward had a complex multi-phased life:

Son

Æthelred II and she married in spring 1002 and the first born of their coupling was Edward, born at Islip, Oxfordshire, probably in 1005, but maybe a bit earlier. His childhood was spent with his sister Godgifu (Goda) and younger brother Alfred in the care of his mother Emma, whilst his older half-siblings, including Edmund who would be called Ironside, children of Æthelred's first wife, some of whom were much the same age as Emma, were already in roles as young adult princes or princesses of the realm or in the care of their grandmother. Six brothers had precedence over Edward. In essence they had separate upbringings as two families.

Emma was a Norman princess, sister of Duke Richard II of Normandy and the marriage was aimed at consolidating a Norman alliance to help keep Viking raids from the shore of England. Richard II would have dearly liked a nephew to be King of England, which might be possible if the offspring of Emma took precedence over her predecessor's children.

All did not go well with the anti-Viking plan thanks to Æthelred's paranoid idea to expel Danes who had settled in England, which only provoked more attacks. As soon as 1003 there was dissent between the Duke and King concerning continuing Viking ease of access to Normandy. And worse, an English fleet, pursuing a group of Vikings who had raided Wessex and were heading to sell their booty in Normandy, attacked Val-de-Saire on the Cotentin peninsula.

Gradually Viking raids escalated, including raids into Kent and along the Sussex coast, and culminated in an invasion by King Sweyn of Denmark. Emma and her three children, all potential heirs to the kingdom of England by descent from the Wessex royal line, fled to Normandy in 1014 when Sweyn rampaged into England and seized the crown by conquest. Emma went first with the Abbot of Peterborough, and the children followed with the Bishop of London. They briefly returned when Æthelred was asked back after Sweyn's unforeseen death, but then fled back again after Sweyn's son, Cnut, reinvaded. It is recorded that Edward came back from Normandy – with the advance party when Æthelred was asked back – and there is a record in the *Saga of St Ólaf* in the *Heimskringla* concerning the life of Ólaf Haraldsson which says that, after the death of Æthelred, Edmund Ironside and Edward had co-reigned, and that Edward fought alongside Edmund defending London, against Cnut. This is possible, but Edward would have been only about thirteen at that time and the *Heimskringla* which is originally an oral history may not be reliable. Finally, Cnut and Edmund reached a stalemate and briefly shared rule in England, Edmund in Wessex and Cnut in the north, midlands and east. But Edmund was dead by the end of 1017 and Cnut was king of all England. Only one full brother of Edmund survived, called Eadwig. All his other full brothers had pre-deceased him. Cnut banished Eadwig, but he foolishly returned, and Cnut had him executed. Edward was now the true blood-line heir of England and knew it, but the teenager dared not return. His mother suffered another fate: Cnut reached an accord with Normandy and 'had her fetched' to become his second wife, a clever political move.

Exile

Thus started the next phase of Edward's life. As nephews of Duke Richard II of Normandy, Edward and Alfred were then brought up in the ducal court, closely observing the rule of uncle Richard II and then of cousin Robert, whom they regarded as a brother. Their sister Godgifu in time married Count Drogo of Mantes. Throughout neither Edward, nor his Norman relatives, would ever forget that he was the true blood-line heir of England and later he was sometimes called 'king' Edward.

The brothers had many kinsmen in Normandy, continued to learn statecraft as potential kings of England, and were treated as sons by their uncle Duke Richard. Duke Robert was looked upon as a 'blood brother'. But there is no record of their having been given estates or proposed in marriage, although Edward witnessed some charters of Duke Robert I before the duke went on his fateful crusade, interestingly signing as 'Edward rex'.

The Athelings Edward and Alfred probably moved around between courts, met many people and had many debts, both personal and monetary, to repay in the future. In his early days in Normandy, Edward spent time travelling around monasteries and may have sworn an oath on Christmas day 1016 to restore in the future some lost lands in the vicinity of London to the Abbey of St Peter and Paul at Ghent, signing as Edward, son of Æthelred. Around the same time, Emma and/or Richard II were obtaining the manor of Rameslie in easstern Sussex from Cnut for Fécamp Abbey, an abbey of special relevance to the ducal family.

Both Edward and Alfred would occasionally sign further Norman charters as noted above, indicating their continued presence in elevated strata of Norman life. Much later, possibly around 1033, 'King' Edward made a forward charter of lands in England, possibly including Old Romney, to the Abbey of Mont-Saint-Michel, to be given once he was king. It is thought that Duke William used this created precedent to promise lands in England to his followers in 1066.

Contender

The next phase of Edward and Alfred's lives began between 1030 and 1035. Robert's relationship with Cnut had deteriorated and he had repudiated a marriage deal with a widowed sister of Cnut called Margaret/Estrith. Robert said, 'she was hateful to him'. For complicated reasons associated with struggles over his own inheritance, Robert considered that it was time that he assisted his 'blood brothers' to regain theirs. Sometime the Norman court had decided to promote Edward as 'King Edward'. Robert started sending envoys to Cnut complaining about the long exile of the brothers. Cnut at first did nothing and Robert assembled a battle fleet to invade England on behalf of the Athelings. As it crossed the Channel a storm blew up and forced the fleet to Jersey. It became impossible to proceed and Robert ordered the fleet to Mont-Saint-Michel where he used the fleet and a further land army to attack Count Alain II of Brittany who was disputing his authority. William of Jumièges says envoys then arrived at the Norman court from Cnut saying that he was gravely ill and would share his kingdom with the Athelings. But for unknown reasons Robert postponed following through on this and went on pilgrimage to Jerusalem. This extraordinary story is supported by charters. The follow- up to this is that in 1035 both Robert of Normandy and Cnut died, Robert from an illness contracted at Nicaea when on his way back from a pilgrimage to the Holy Land and Cnut in November from his terminal illness. A big opportunity had been lost.

In England a tussle for the throne commenced between Harold Harefoot, dubious son of Cnut by his first marriage and Harthacnut, his son by Emma and the Athelings half-brother. This is described in the previous chapter. Other attempts by the Athelings to participate in the English kingmaking – one by Edward to land near Southampton and link up with his mother at Winchester and another by Alfred from Flanders both failed, with the horrible death of Alfred.

When Harthacnut finally became king, he and Emma, prompted by Godwin and others, invited Edward to join them in 1041 as co-ruler or heir presumptive. When Harthacnut died in 1042, Edward was in prime position to regain the throne for the Wessex line.

Rightful King

The champion of Edward in the Witan was Earl Godwin of Wessex, and he was also supported by other southern magnates and bishops. Earls Leofric of Mercia and Siward of Northumbria who leaned more to a Scandinavian outlook took somewhat longer to make up their minds. But eventually the direct blood line from Wessex created the strongest argument. Edward (to become 'the Confessor') was eventually crowned at Winchester on Easter Day, 3 April 1043, nearly ten months after the death of Harthacnut. This may have been a deliberate delay to associate the crowning of Edward with one of the most Holy days.

Edward's mother had behaved in a very strange way, which has never been adequately explained, suggesting Magnus of Norway as king of England, and holding on to the state treasures. Her relationship with Edward appears to have been a cold one, and possibly stemmed back to her lack of regard for Æthelred II, plus a perceived lack of support for her earlier schemes from Edward. Perhaps she saw a frailty in Edward. The Witan finally decided, and Edward was eventually crowned. Soon afterwards the treasures were removed from Emma, and she was left to live out the rest of her life quietly at Winchester until she died in 1052.

Soon afterwards King Edward declared that land at Steyning was to pass to

Fécamp Abbey after the death of Bishop Ælfwine. Harmer thought that this might have been a dubious charter, but it is noted that Harold Godwinson was later to seize this land for his own (although he never touched Rameslie).

Edward was strongly supported from the start of his reign by the Godwin family. There were almost immediate post-coronation challenges from Scandinavia which lasted several years. Magnus planned an invasion, but was held up by fighting with another Sweyn, a cousin of the Godwinsons, over Denmark. Sweyn pulled the Godwin card and asked for help from Edward but was ignored. Sweyn was eventually chased out, and Magnus started to prepare his plans for England once more, only to die in late 1047. Sweyn returned, was re-crowned, and remained King of Denmark, and held it (just) against Harald Hardrada who had taken Norway (but who was to die at the Battle of Stamford Bridge in 1066), until he too died in 1074.

Once more in 1048 there were Viking raids on England against Thanet, Sandwich and the Isle of Wight, all of which were chased off by Edward's innovative navy, by now a navy based on southern ports including Hastings, Pevensey, Rye and Winchelsea, which provided crews as needed rather than having an expensive standing navy crewed by mercenaries. The towns were given some privileges in exchange. This was the forerunner of the Cinque Ports. In 1049 Edward assisted the Emperor Henry III in his war against Baldwin V of Flanders, by using the English navy to blockade the Channel. No doubt many ships from Hastings and the other future Cinque Ports took part in these actions.

Revolt

In the early years of his rule Edward had brought in Normans to advise and assist him. He also needed to keep the English great earls, Siward, Leofric and Godwin on side, which was either helped or hindered by the earls' rivalries. Godwin rose to be much more influential than the others and, possibly to appease him, Edward married his daughter Edith in 1045. But there were very clearly great tensions between the King and his father-in-law about the Norman influence. Normans and Norman abbeys had received grants of land from Edward and Edward's nephew, Ralf of Mantes, became earl of an area centred on Hereford. Tensions continued to rise. Two events in 1051 – the advancement of Robert Champart of Jumièges, who had already been made Bishop of London, to the archbishopric of Canterbury over Godwin's candidate, and a secondary event involving Eustace of Boulogne caused a complete rift. After an armed stand-off and near civil war, and with the support of Earls Siward and Leofric, Edward banished Godwin and his family, and Queen Edith was sent to a convent. These were extraordinary events. It can only be assumed that Edward had become almost completely dependent on Godwin but actually detested him, possibly because of his role in killing his brother Alfred, but also because of his rising opposition to Edward's wishes. Edward had taken his first clear opportunity to rid himself of the Godwins, who to some extent had operated as his family. He must also have considered divorcing Edith as the couple remained childless.

What happened in the year to change things so dramatically? Was it a possible visit of Duke William II to England in 1051 and/or an indication to William via Robert Champart that he might be nominated by Edward as his preferred inheritor of the English throne the root cause of all this? If so, this might have been conditional on Edward having no child to inherit or no other Wessex blood-line relative being found – although William and Edward were related via the Norman ducal line, they were not related via the Wessex line. William may have overinterpreted this position. We just don't fully know – records are contradictory, and much academic controversy has flowed over the issues.

Restitution of the Godwins

The Godwins had regrouped in both Flanders and Ireland. It was not long before they started probing to return. In June 1052 Godwin made a sortie from Flanders to see what support he could raise in Wessex. Edward's fleet sallied from Sandwich to meet him, but a storm blew up and Godwin was forced westwards and he 'acquired' some more ships from Pevensey before sailing back to Bruges. He then returned to the Isle of Wight where he met up with Harold and Leofwine Godwinson who had nine ships full of mercenaries from Ireland. Godwin re-imposed his authority at Portland and sailed east again gathering men and ships, willingly or otherwise, from ports including Hastings, Rye, Old Romney and Dover as he went. He eventually arrived at London, where he persuaded the citizens to support him. Edward called for reinforcements, but Earls Siward and Leofric were noticeable by their absence, a truce was made, and the Witan called. Godwin cleared himself on oath of involvement in Alfred Atheling's death and of treasonable intent by himself and his family. But Edward was able to take Godwin's youngest son Wulfnoth and his grandson by Sweyn, Hákon as hostage to Godwin's future good behaviour. The Witan decided that the crisis of 1052 had been caused by 'bad counsellors' – that is Edward's Norman friends and advisors.

Queen Edith was released from her convent, thoughts of divorce removed and the Norman Archbishop of Canterbury, Robert Champart, was sent packing to Normandy, somehow, it is believed, taking Edward's hostages Wulfnoth and Hákon with him. Godwin's protégé Stigand was inserted into Canterbury in Champart's stead. Stigand was promptly excommunicated by the Pope, both as a usurper and also for plurality (holding on to other ecclesiastical appointments in addition to Canterbury). He could not consecrate bishops, nor could he crown kings. This situation was maintained by successive popes and William of Normandy would exploit it later.

The Godwins were firmly established back in power and were now truly difficult to dislodge. Earl Godwin died in 1053 and Harold Godwinson became the pre-eminent earl, taking over Wessex, with East Anglia being transferred to Ælfgar, son of Leofric. In 1055 Earl Siward died and Harold's brother Tostig became earl of Northumbria. Finally, in 1057 Leofric of Mercia died, handing the earldom to his son Ælfgar. Ralf, earl of Hereford, a possible claimant to the English throne as the son of Edward's sister Godgifu, also died in the same year. Harold promptly added the lands of Ralf's earldom to Wessex. East Anglia, which Ælfgar had previously held, went to his brother Gyrth Godwinson, and another brother Leofwine Godwinson took over Buckinghamshire and Kent and the area in between. So virtually every earldom south of the old Danelaw line, plus Northumbria, was held by a son of Earl Godwin.

The *Anglo-Saxon Chronicle* confirms that the king remained in good health. The names of people associated with the court become more Scandinavian, although French names did not totally disappear. Most in the church had English names. The role of Queen Edith probably increased, and it is believed that she stirred up hostility to Earl Ælfgar of Mercia, who was banished. But then Ælfgar caused mayhem around the southern Welsh Marches having allied with the king of north Wales. Fortunately for him, he was able to regain his earldom through diplomacy. Edith may have also been implicated in some of Tostig Godwinson's less savoury adventures. Edwin, eldest son of Ælfgar, took over Mercia on his father's death in 1062.

There were tensions between the Godwinson brothers, but as long as they co-operated and worked with, and nominally under, the king, the realm was strong. Foreign affairs were also surprisingly stable. The policy towards Wales and Scotland was defensive. Sweyn of Denmark was first cousin to the Godwinsons, and the King was related to Duke William II of Normandy. Tostig was married to Judith of Flanders, daughter of Baldwin IV and Eleanor of Normandy, a granddaughter of Richard II. Judith's niece was Matilda of Flanders who would marry Duke William II of Normandy.

Death of Godwin

Earl Godwin died in 1053 and Harold Godwinson became the pre-eminent earl, taking over Wessex. King Edward was happy to delegate military and other major issues to Harold and his brother Tostig. We are told that he spent much time praying and hunting. The *Vita Ædwardi Regis*, which is a strange document with Godwinian overtones, implies that before 1052 Edward was misguided, and that after this everything went well. The *ASC* confirms that the King remained in good health. Although there remained many tensions in England eastern Sussex and Wessex appear to have been generally outside the frays after this.

In late 1054 Edward may have gifted to Fécamp Abbey some land, houses and salterns around Eastbourne and Pevensey, which might have irritated Harold – who had previously usurped the manor of Steyning in west Sussex from Fécamp and would have dearly loved to have obtained the manor of Rameslie, still held by the Norman abbey, to boost his presence in eastern Sussex, which was definitely weaker than further west, as we have seen above.

Succession

More importantly, in the continued absence of children, Edward had started to think about his successor again and tried to find Edward, the son of Edmund Ironside, who had fled with his family to Hungary. Bishop Ealdred of Worcester set out in 1054 to track him down but was unsuccessful. In 1056 Harold, in diplomat mode, may have travelled to visit Baldwin of Flanders and on to Cologne then to Regensburg, met the Hungarian king there, found Edward and negotiated his return to England as a possible heir for King Edward. Walker proposes a scenario for this, but it is not directly recorded. Whatever happened, Edward arrived in England with his family in 1057, coinciding with the death of Earl Leofric. Edward died soon after arriving, but he had a young son, Edgar, and other children whom king Edward took into the royal household.

Edward ensured that Edgar was looked after as if his own son, and he was designated Edgar Atheling, as he was of the Wessex blood line and the grandson of Edward's older half-brother Edmund Ironside. Edward may have required an oath to recognise this status. The title was clearly used on ceremonial occasions. In the *Liber Vitae* or *Book of Life* of New Minster, Winchester, the names of King Edward, Queen Edith and Edgar Atheling are entered as a group. At that time Athelings had a specific legal footing, second only to the king and equivalent to an archbishop. Edward also started to strengthen Edgar's position. He granted him lands and titles and his sister Margaret was betrothed to Malcolm of Scotland.

Both Bates and Licence refer to what is a little-known record at this time from the *Chronicle of the Abbey of Saint Riquier*, in Ponthieu. This abbey had been founded in about 625 and later held lands in Norfolk. Their Abbot Gervin I (d.1075) had visited Edwards's court. One of his monk's, Hariulf, wrote in their Chronicle that

> after Edward's death that an earl called Harold had usurped the English throne in contempt of the oath which he had made to the late king to cede the kingdom to Edgar.

The importance of this is that the record was made outside of both Normandy and England in a pretty neutral place and had not been subjected to any redaction. Retrospectively, it can also be noted that *ASC* (*D*) for the year 1066 records after the description of the slaughter on the field at a place to be called Battle:

> Archbishop Ealdred and the garrison in London wanted to have Prince Edgar for king, just as was his natural right.

Although this was safely written after Harold was killed it shows that Edgar's right was clearly known. If Edgar's right to the kingdom was so widely known and if Harold and no doubt many others had made the oath to support Edgar it now puts subsequent events into a somewhat different perspective.

Harold's 'Fishing Trip'

Earl Harold Godwinson took a sea trip on the English Channel in the late spring or early summer of 1064. The outcome of this voyage may have led to a key point, even the deciding factor, in William the Conqueror's decision to invade England after the death of Edward the Confessor, and the crowning of Harold as King of England in very early January 1066.

The voyage is one of the great mysteries of the complex preludes to the Battle of Hastings on 14th October 1066. Just why did Earl Harold Godwinson take three ships from Bosham in West Sussex, and end up by chance or intention in the feudal county of Ponthieu, which lay between Normandy and Flanders on the other side of the Channel? There he was 'welcomed' by Count Guy I of Ponthieu, taken to his castle at Beaurain-sur-Canche and maybe held hostage. Later he was passed to the 'care' of William, Duke of Normandy, before he was eventually allowed to return to England.

What were the possible causes for the trip, what were Duke William's relationships with Guy of Ponthieu and his family, and reactions and events in Ponthieu and Normandy up until the time that Harold was met by Duke William and escorted to Rouen?

The end of the voyage to Ponthieu is immortalised with imagery on the Bayeux Tapestry (BT) with the associated words:

> HIC: APPREHENDIT: WIDO: HAROLDVM: ET DVXIT: EVM AD BELREM: ET IBI EVM: TENVIT – here Guy (Wido) seized Harold and led him to Beaurain (Belrem) and there he held him.

About Ponthieu

Ponthieu was not a part of Normandy, but Guy had become a vassal lord of William's after the Battle of Mortemer in 1054 (see below). There is no doubt that Guy had a family history of antagonism with William, which dated back to William's disagreements with Guy's uncle, Count William of Arques, whom the young duke had created a count sometime between 1042–4. William of Arques (also of Talou) was the son of Duke Richard II of Normandy by Papia. His older half-brothers were dukes of Normandy: Richard III from 1026 to 1027, and Robert I from 1027 to 1035. Robert I was the father of William the Conqueror. In 1035, following the death of Duke Robert I, William of Arques had challenged his young nephew William's right to succeed his father, basing his own claim on a legitimate descent from Richard II. There was therefore more than a little angst between the two Williams.

Arques had withdrawn from William's siege of Domfront in 1051–2, renounced his vassalage and went off to rebel in eastern Normandy, having already subverted the Duke's garrison at the castle of Arques (now Arques-la-Bataille near Dieppe). William of Arques was joined in his revolt by his brother-in-law, Enguerrand II, who in 1052 had become Count of Ponthieu. To make familial matters worse, Enguerrand had once been married to Duke William's sister Adelaide, part of whose dowry had been the small county of Aumale, next to Ponthieu. This marriage had been childless and was annulled on the grounds of consanguinity in 1049–50. Aumale had reverted to the over-lordship of Duke William. Loss of land was never well received by the Norman aristocracy.

This led to a siege of the castle of Arques by Duke William. In an attempt to relieve the siege, King Henry of France arranged a small armed force to try to do so but forces loyal to Duke William ambushed them at nearby Saint-Aubin-sur-Scie on 25 October 1053. In the skirmish the disgruntled Enguerrand, who was part of the raiding group was killed.

Figure 44. Arques-la-Bataille Castle, near Dieppe. From Google Earth

Duke William duly recovered the castle of Arques and banished William of Arques from Normandy, and Guy I (either son or brother of Enguerrand) became Count of Ponthieu. Following this episode Guy was involved with King Henry of France in early 1054 in an aggressive thrust by the King into Normandy from the east, which resulted in a victory at the Battle of Mortemer for Duke William's forces. Guy was taken prisoner and held at Bayeux for two years until he swore perpetual fealty to Duke William, with the promise to supply him with the services of 100 soldiers each year. So, they became nominal allies, but begrudgingly, and it has been noted that Guy continued signing charters of the French king.

In 1056 Guy attended a meeting in Saint-Omer arranged by Count Baldwin V of Flanders, which was also attended by Harold Godwinson and Guy of Amiens, who later wrote the *Carmen de Hastingae Proelio*. At the time Harold was visiting Baldwin, perhaps whilst en route to, or returning from, a visit to Rome. One of the results of this meeting is that on 13 November 1056, Baldwin V of Flanders approved a diploma for the Abbey of Saint Peter and St Paul of Ghent, and among the witnesses were Earl Harold Godwinson and Count Guy of Ponthieu.

This was also a time of a flurry of diplomatic activity and jockeying for position in Europe following the death of Holy Roman Emperor Henry III. As a side event of this there may have been some involvement of Harold in negotiations for the return of Edmund Ironsides's son, Edward, to England as a potential heir to Edward the Confessor. Edward had been sent to Sweden by King Cnut after the death of Edmund Ironside. He then made his way somehow to the Hungarian royal court. He returned with his family to the English royal court in 1057 having been found by Edward the Confessor's emissaries. Unfortunately he died soon afterwards, leaving a son Edgar Atheling and two daughters. One daughter, Margaret, later became the second wife of King Malcolm III of Scotland, and their daughter Maud/Matilda would marry Henry I of England in 1100, bringing the blood line of Wessex back into the English succession.

Variations on a theme

Gade has suggested, from her very interesting review of the Norwegian sources for the events of the Conquest, that Harold may also have been trying to secure the early release of his brother Wulfnoth and nephew Hákon from Normandy, who were being held hostage 'in the care of' William on behalf of King Edward, following the Godwin-led near civil war in England in 1051. She also raises the 'flexibly logical' suggestion that this event might have been somehow conflated with the later records concerning Harold's time in Normandy in 1064 and its objectives. This was seeing Harold in diplomatic mode, ten years before the Confessor's death, and maybe long before he might have even considered that one day he might be king of England himself.

This is just one of many attempts which have been made to understand just why Harold made this fateful voyage in the late spring or early summer of 1064, the full complexities of his subsequent 'entertainment' by Duke William, and the rationale and the nature of his voyage and sojourn at Beaurain-sur-Canche (the 'Belrem' of the BT, now called Beaurainville). The true story remains obscure and this very obscurity gives rise to many ambiguous conspiracy theories and was part of the Norman hagiographers' starting point to justify William's claim to the throne of England.

There are more varying stories, preceding 1064, concerning the manoeuvres to secure a clear blood-line successor to Edward the Confessor in the person of Edward Atheling, son of Edmund Ironside (Edward the Confessor's half-brother). As we have seen above, Hariulf of Saint-Riquier suggests that Edward obtained an oath from English magnates to recognise Edgar's right to succeed, perhaps in 1062/3. This is rarely mentioned. Against him William also had an undisputed but indirect female blood-line claim via his great-aunt Queen Emma, who was the mother of Edward the Confessor from her marriage to King Æthelred II. But he had no Wessex blood. And in the shadowy wings waited some potential Scandinavian claimants, distantly related to King Cnut, wishing to reclaim the lost Danish English kingdom. Harold was not of royal blood, but his sister Edith was married to Edward.

But turning back to further explanations of the voyage, we know that both William of Jumièges and William of Poitiers claim that Harold was on a mission on behalf of King Edward the Confessor to promise the succession of the throne of England to William. The so-called briefing meeting between Edward and Harold is the first illustration of the Bayeux Tapestry. This ambivalent meeting, as shown, fits the Norman stories, but it may not have happened as imagined. The context of the meeting, according to the mainly Norman sources, was associated with the dynastic succession to the English throne, and was a follow up to the meeting between William and Edward in 1051–2, as reported in the *D* version of the *Anglo-Saxon Chronicle*, when Edward may have promised his throne to William, as long as there was no more direct blood line successor (at that time it was possible that Edward might have children). To have done more would have subverted the right of the English Witan to elect the successor. Morillo gives a concise selection of these sources and he also includes a paper on naval logistics in 1066, much of which is pertinent to any voyage at that time across the Channel (see below).

A further conspiracy theory exists, suggested to the author by his colleague, Neil Clephane-Cameron, which sees Harold 'set-up' by Edward with an ostensibly bona fide diplomatic mission in order for William to apprehend him, but a Channel storm added an unanticipated twist, to which William, with his accustomed adaptability, was able to respond for his own long-term, strategic benefit.

Another theory exists that, for diplomatic or his personal reasons, Harold may have been seeking a new wife from either Flanders or Normandy, rather than the one proposed at that time – Ealdgyth, widow of the dead king of North Wales and sister of the northern earls Edwin and Morcar – which would have had English strategic benefits, but may not have totally fitted Harold's plans.

Eadmer says that King Edward told Harold that in going to the continent against his advice that Harold would bring 'dishonour on the kingdom and discredit to himself'. And William of Malmesbury simply envisioned that Harold went fishing and was blown seriously off course.

Harold being at his country-seat at Boseham, went for recreation on board a fishing boat, and, for the purpose of prolonging his sport, put out to sea;

when a sudden tempest arising, he was driven with his companions on the coast of Ponthieu.

It is difficult to believe that he was just going on a 'jolly' or fishing trip and, if so, why did he take three ships full of armed men? One can be fairly sure that he normally left the business of fishing to poor fishermen. Sea voyages could be fraught with danger and were usually not undertaken lightly, especially by kings and earls of the realm, unless there was a particularly good reason. And if a tempest had blown up near Bosham surely they would have tried to run into one of the English harbours in Sussex, including Pevensey, Hastings and Winchelsea, rather than allow themselves to be blown 160km (100miles) to Ponthieu?

The BT's first scene is of Harold being 'briefed' by the Confessor before preparing for his voyage. This unsurprisingly fits the Norman storylines, but is, as noted above, ambiguous. Did Edward, if he advised Harold at all, ask him to visit William on a diplomatic mission to find out what William was thinking, and did he tell him not to try to secure the release of Godwin family hostages still held by William (on Edward's behalf) following the Godwin family's insurrection in 1051? What was he going to talk about if Edgar was the de facto heir, to whom Harold and others has sworn an oath of succession? Was Edward actually sending Harold to inform William of his decision to nominate Edgar as his successor? As the most powerful earl, Harold would have been ideally suited to say to William, 'Look, even I have accepted this'. William then decides that here is a potential ally (both having had their ambitions displaced) and subsequently offers Harold the opportunity to retain his power if he will support William to the throne (perhaps even in a joint kingdom per the earlier Wessex/Scandinavian examples) and obtains Harold's oath to this, per the BT.

Wulfnoth, the youngest son of Earl Godwin and youngest brother of Harold, and Godwin's grandson Hákon, son of Harold's dead brother Sweyn, had been transferred by Edward to William's 'care' after the Godwin rebellion. On his final return to England in 1065 Harold did bring back his nephew Hákon, perhaps as a sign of William's good faith, but his youngest brother Wulfnoth remained in William's 'care', a continuing hostage to fortune, retained as hostage for Harold's good faith. Edward may have been only too happy to leave the hostages in Normandy for insurance against the powerful Godwins.

Was Harold not aiming for Normandy at all and going on a diplomatic mission to Flanders on behalf of Edward? He had made similar trips before. Flanders was as large as Normandy at that time and its coastline extended to south of Boulogne. The Flemish were reasonably good allies of the English and friendly to the Godwins (Tostig Godwinson was married to Baldwin IV's daughter Judith, and Flanders had provided a refuge for the Godwins in 1051) so could be helpful in deterring further Danish invasion intentions, which were not improbable.

Sailing the English Channel

The English Channel can be a difficult place to sail, with its strong tidal range and currents, as well as having somewhat unpredictable weather. William was to find this when he first set out with his invasion fleet from Dives, near Caen on or about 13th September 1066 and was beset by strong westerly winds between Dives and Saint-Valéry-sur-Somme, losing numbers of ships, men and supplies en route.

Below is a map of the eastern English Channel. On it are marked routes to Boulogne (Flanders, in red); Le Touquet (Ponthieu, blue), Dieppe (Normandy, white) and Harfleur (Normandy at the mouth of the Seine, green). These take absolutely no account of winds, tides, shoals, sandbanks, or sea-cliffs. It would have taken some time to sail across, much more time than the few hours on a modern ferry. William's invasion fleet, once it set off again, departed with a favourable wind on 27th or 28th September 1066, and took about 12 hours to do a shorter crossing from Saint-Valéry-sur-Somme to Pevensey, about 2/3rds the distance of any of the above sailings (William's crossing is shown on the map for comparison in purple).

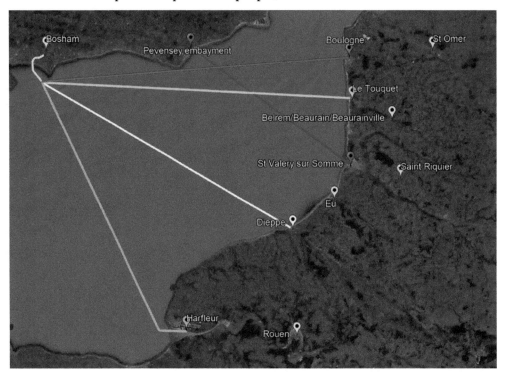

Figure 45. Various straight-line routes from Bosham to possible destinations. Sailing across the Channel requires constant directional changes to allow for tidal flows and windage, so these routes are representational only. Also marked are key places mentioned in the dialogue and for comparison William's invasion route from Saint-Valéry-sur-Somme to Pevensey. Baseline map from Google Earth

During a sail across the Channel the tidal flow may change direction twice or more, with the outflowing (falling) tide to the Atlantic taking ships westwards and the incoming (rising) tide pushing them towards the North Sea. Big wind directional shifts and strength changes can occur during 24–30 hours. Ships in 1064 were poor at sailing into the wind, so wind strengthening from the west could push a boat in the eastern English Channel towards Dover, a big wind-shift to a strong easterly could push a ship back towards Brittany. For more technical information about sailing Viking type ships, see the Viking Ship Museum website.

We have no idea of either the precise date of Harold's trip which ended at Ponthieu – the date of which would enable accurate tidal calculations – or the actual weather conditions, which are totally unknowable, during the voyage. The ploughing and sowing scene on the lower border of the *BT* at the point after Harold and Guy's conversation may indicate that it was around March or April. But we can note that the predominant winds in the Channel for most of the year are from the west. So, if the destination was the Seine it would have taken a very considerable 'blow' to push the ships so far off course to Ponthieu therefore, in logical terms, this enhances the probability that the intended destination was Flanders. It is interesting that the *BT* shows the three ships arriving together: surely if there had been a storm they would have been scattered? But overall this analysis takes us nowhere in deciding exactly where Harold's ships were aiming for, unless he was in fact deliberately aiming for Ponthieu yet missed a good harbour and ran aground on one of the many sandbanks around that coast. The question then is: 'Why Ponthieu?'

In Ponthieu

So far so unsatisfactory. We can definitely concur with all previous analyses that really we have no idea at all, apart from informed guesses, of why Harold made this journey, whether it was sanctioned by King Edward or not, if it was a ruse, and where he actually intended to go. If the desired destination was any of Normandy, Ponthieu or Flanders, was the visit a surprise one or flagged in advance to William, Guy or Baldwin V, any two of these, or all three?

Today it would seem very strange for the most politically powerful person in one country to make an unarranged visit to a foreign country. In those days it might have been downright dangerous, as the citizens of every coastal town along either side of the English Channel were used to repelling piratical raids with lethal force without asking questions first, and to ransoming, even enslaving, shipwrecked sailors. So given the circumstances as shown in the *BT* it does appear that this was an unrequested or uninvited visit to Ponthieu, or even if pre-arranged, could Guy of Ponthieu have seen a sneaky opportunity to get back some money and land from William?

In the *BT* we see Harold wading ashore to be met on the beach by Count Guy and his retainers, possibly near St. Valéry-sur-Somme, where there is a big estuary, or between Étaples and Le Touquet where there is the estuary of the Canche river. There appears to be minimal manhandling with the companions of Harold keeping their arms ready but still sheathed and the apprehender of Harold disarming him and pointing to Guy as if to say, 'Do you know who this is?' A pointing finger from Guy identifies Harold, but also suggests that it might be a good idea for Harold just to turn around and go back to sea. As a side-line it can be noted that there are two men in the lower border of the BT at this point, one looking backwards at some deer and the other forwards. Each wield two clubs or swords and they have a pack of hunting dogs. Were they the ones who spotted Harold's landing and called for help?

Figure 46. Harold's landing and apprehension. Image extract from Bruce

Eventually all travelled inland the 26km (16miles) or so via the Canche valley to Belrem/Beaurain-sur-Canche, with lances still shouldered and no swords drawn, with both Harold and Guy carrying a hawk (the significance of which in the *BT* is that this indicated that they were lords). The small town is 10km (6 miles) south-east of Montreuil-sur-Mer and is now called Beaurainville. Its castle was on the edge of the settlement and the 40m (130ft) high 'motte feodale' of Beaurain castle can still be visited. It is a steep-sided, heavily wooded, knoll. An illustration by Adrien de Montigny of the castle (dated 1610) showed a bailey and curtain wall with flanking towers with the motte topped by a two-story brick building, probably replacing an earlier stone donjon. There is no brick or stone to be seen now, just the motte, the last stones having been used in the construction of a water mill in 1822.

The meeting illustrated in the *BT* is of course a Norman interpretation. Unless Harold was expected, there would be no reason for Guy to be waiting nearby to meet him on the beach. Maybe the huntsmen had raised the alarm and Guy's troops had gone to see what all the fuss was about, perhaps rubbing their hands in anticipation of a juicy ransom. Whatever happened, Harold and his party ended up in the castle at Beaurain. Once recognised as a high-ranking nobleman he would, as etiquette demanded, have been handled with some respect but he was still a (possibly unexpected) foreigner in a strange land. As we have seen above, Guy and Harold had met before and had no known reason to dislike each other, although Harold was the more powerful man.

There would have been little to be gained from an English alliance with Guy, but Guy may have had valuable information that Harold could benefit from and he could have been being used as an intermediary, although his behaviour in possibly demanding a ransom would suggest otherwise – unless it was a double bluff or a win-win set up.

In the *BT* we see Harold and Guy having a discussion in Guy's castle. The English have their weapons back, but the sword belts are unbuckled, and the swords are sheathed and pointed to the ground. A man is seen watching the discussion from behind a column to the right of Guy, and this implies that he will soon run off to get a message to William. This may have been a messenger waiting to be sent to William, a simple sneak after reward, an Englishman who had escaped and then somehow crossed 60km of Ponthieu undetected to get to Normandy, or a Norman spy.

The Handover

Although Beaurainville is 60km from the Normandy/Ponthieu border just north of Eu, it is 160km (100 miles) overall to Rouen where William is known to have been at that time (*BT*). So it would have taken some time, even with fast horses, to get the message to William. The messengers may have taken at least one Englishman with them as an Englishman (with the moustache) is seen pleading with William to send messengers back to negotiate and do a deal, or simply to send people to collect Harold and his party and escort them to Normandy. Chronicles indicate that William eventually paid a large sum of money and gave Guy some land (possibly a fraction of his county's losses at Aumale), to hand Harold over him over. This may not have been a ransom, but a gift of thanks. The exchange eventually took place at Eu, 68km (52 miles) from Beaurainville, where William went to welcome Harold.

It is noted in the *BT* that Guy is shown riding a mule for this trip, maybe a mocking gesture by the designer or embroiderer to this vassal lord who dared do a deal with William. Above the transaction scene there are two camels in the upper border of the *BT*, a truly exotic animal in northern Europe at that time. These must have had relevant symbolism, as does much of the upper and lower borders of the *BT*, in this case probably biblical and connected to large matters of 'justice, mercy, and faithfulness'. This is related to those who are scrupulous about small things but ignore higher issues.

> Woe unto you, scribes and Pharisees, hypocrites! For you pay tithe of mint and anise and cummin, and have omitted the weightier matters of the law, justice, mercy, and faith: these ought you to have done, and not to leave the other undone; who strain at a gnat and swallow a camel. (Matthew 23: vv 23 and 24)

The upper and lower borders of the *Bayeux Tapestry* are filled with classical, eastern and Christian allegories and real life scenes, with mythological figures, such as wyverns, griffins, winged horses, dragons, as well as (amongst others) lions, tigers, camels, peacocks, bears, fish, eels, dogs, birds, plus farming and hunting scenes, pastiche illustrations of Aesop's and others' fables, as well Halley's comet and scenes of battle and erotica, not unlike moralistic scenes carved in early Romanesque churches. Amongst the identified fables are: The fox and the crow; the wolf and the lamb; the wolf and the crane; the wolf and the kid; the frog, the mouse and the hawk. The first is repeated three times with the piece of cheese being dropped by the crow varying in position (it's once in mid-air!), the symbolism being believed to represent the tug of war between William (the crow) and Harold (the fox) with the piece of cheese they both want representing England. The last is a tale of false friends – this picture re-appears in Tina Greene's *The Battle Tapestry*.

William and Harold then went to Rouen and the next major episodes of the interactions of William and Harold, as told by the *BT* and Norman scribes, were played out to the climax at the field of Hastings. These are another story.

Figure 47. Guy transfers Harold to the care of William. Image extract from Bruce

Final thoughts

Concerning the story of 'the fishing trip', it clearly has much ambiguity and has been variously over interpreted over the years. What has been done above is to try to put the whole story in its contexts and to make and query yet more alternatives.

A final word about Guy: it has been suggested that Guy of Ponthieu was a 'Companion of William' at the Battle of Hastings, but the only mention of him in any of the major Companion lists is one solitary entry, 'Gui, Comte de Ponthieu', in the 1931 *Falaise Roll* extra list, 865 years after the event, and must be regarded as dubious. Maybe he sent his 100 soldiers, but he does not appear in *Domesday Book*, which suggests that he never received lands in England, the normal prize of a Companion. The *Carmen de Hastingae Proelio* mentions an 'heir of Ponthieu' at the Battle of Hastings. As Guy had no son this must have been his daughter Agnes' husband – born in about

1030. Count Guy I died in 1100 and was succeeded by his daughter, who had married Robert of Bellême, 3rd Earl of Shrewsbury and Count of Alençon, who continued the family feud and supported William's son, Robert Curthose, against William after 1077 and against William II Rufus after William's death. Entries similar to 'Belville' but not Alençon are found in three of the major Companions lists.

Wulfnoth was, of course, fated to remain in Normandy until William's death, after which he was briefly released and returned to England with King William II 'Rufus'. He was then re-confined at Winchester where he died in about 1094. He would have been held in relatively comfortable circumstances and appears to have occasionally been let out to sign charters of William II, including one at Hastings in January 1091, confirming Bishop Osmund's reorganisation at Salisbury Cathedral. This was on one of the several occasions when Rufus was mustering troops at Hastings for a sortie to Normandy to confront his brother, Robert Curthose. Was it still considered too dangerous to leave a Godwinson in England whilst the king fought in Normandy?

Return to England

On his return to England Harold seems to have picked up where he left off, being the right-hand man of Edward. There was a revolt in 1065 against his brother, Earl Tostig, by the Northumbrians. Tostig had increased taxes, never a popular thing to do, but there were deeper-seated reasons for the revolt. He had curbed the power of local landholders through intrigue and murder, and his men were using arbitrary justice to enforce tax collections. In the autumn of 1065 this led the thegns of Northumbria to seize and occupy York and kill Tostig's retainers. The *Anglo-Saxon Chronicle* says that the revolt involved 'all the thegns of Yorkshire'. They took back what they deemed theirs by right, then declared Tostig an outlaw and sent for Morcar, the younger brother of Earl Edwin of Mercia, to be the new earl. Led by 'earl' Morcar they were joined at Northampton by Earl Edwin (Edwin and Morcar were sons of Ælfgar) and moved south looking to find recompense from Tostig's holdings. Harold met them but, after he had discussed the issues with the rebels, he concluded that it was impossible for Tostig to remain Earl of Northumbria.

Harold returned to the king, counselled against military action against Morcar and his thegns, and acceptance of the rebels' demands. Edward was angry, as Tostig had been a favourite, but was finally swayed. For the first time since Sweyn's death, the Godwinsons were divided. Harold went to Northampton and told Morcar he was now officially Earl of Northumbria, and the rebels that they were pardoned. He also probably finalised the arrangement to marry Morcar and Edwin's sister Ealdgyth to strengthen his English alliances and remove any likelihood of a marriage with a Norman or Flemish princess. Tostig continued to argue with King Edward and in the end took himself off to Flanders, before he was exiled. He went to Bruges to join his brother-in-law, count Baldwin V.

In November 1065 it became obvious that King Edward was dying, but just before he passed, he appears to have granted some lands in eastern Sussex to Westminster Abbey. In charters *S1039, S1040* and *S1043* of 1065/66 in the *Telligraphus of Edward* he gives Westminster Abbey lands at … Eastburneham (?Eastbourne, Sussex), Chillington in Eastbourne, and at West Chiltington. These may be forgeries.

Death and Heir

New kings of England were normally drawn from the royal family but not necessarily by primogeniture. The probable heir was Edgar Atheling and, normally, with the approval of the Witan, he might have succeeded with Queen Edith as regent during his minority and with Harold 'Dux Anglorum' continuing as his military aide and advisor, running the country for a few years until the boy was old enough to rule on his own. Edith wished to restore Tostig who was a potential ally of Edgar, who might have been easily manipulated to Harold's disadvantage and even led to Harold's downfall. There were some aggressive claims from Harald Hardrada of Norway and William of Normandy, the latter having the family claim through his great-aunt, Emma of Normandy and consecrated Queen of England.

The meeting of the Witan and celebrations held at Christmas saw all five earls, the archbishops of York and Canterbury, eight bishops and many leading thegns gathered in London. After Christmas many would have left to return to their homes. On 5 January 1066 Edward summoned the Witan to his deathbed, it may have been a somewhat depleted Witan and not very representative of the provinces. He had been semi-conscious for several days but had roused. He is said to have 'commended' his kingdom and the protection of his queen to Harold and bound his Norman servants to take oaths of loyalty to Harold.

Whatever he actually said, the Witan almost immediately afterwards acclaimed Harold King of England and he was crowned in much haste, before anyone could change their minds. We do not know what was said. What has never been clearly ascertained, and probably never will be, is whether Harold had manoeuvred long term for this. The events of the last few months, including the loss of Tostig, may have been the decider for him and the plans he might have for England. He had been Edward's right-hand man, protector, advisor, diplomat and fixer for over ten years: did Edward mean to hand over to him as a caretaker, not as king? Would Harold have been just as content serving Edgar Atheling? He broke an oath to support Edgar and would not have wished to serve William, nor co-rule with William if he had made such a deal in 1064/5. Licence says,

> By taking the throne from Edgar Atheling, Harold changed the rules. William decided that he had as much right as Harold. As an opportunist he did what he could get away with and made up his excuses later.

It could be noted that he had more right than Harold, as he was at least within Edward's extended family via Emma, his mother, and son of Edward's blood-brother, if not by the Wessex blood line.

The story from after early January 1066 is that of the preparations on both sides of the Channel, and of other related events on the North Sea leading up to the Battle of Hastings. Eastern Sussex fitfully slept, watching its coasts, until rudely awakened by William's landing on 28th or 29th September when all hell broke out. But for now, the story is ended.

I commend my kingdom and the protection of my queen to Harold.

Edward the Confessor

10
An End Piece

This small book has explored the many changes across eastern Sussex until 1066, from the dawn of time, and the intrigues involving Harold and William which eventually led to the Battle of Hastings at Battle.. For the author it was like writing from the tip of an iceberg about what lies beneath from scraps of information found carved in the ice under a covering layer of snow, but it is to be hoped that you have found the content of interest and that it has raised a question or three or many more that you might wish to explore. That would not be surprising, as writing about such a period undoubtedly raises more questions than answers, as the accurate sources are so lean in number and sparse in content, idiosyncratic, open to interpretations, and sometimes seemingly just simply weird and semi-mythical. This has not been helped by previous over-dogmatic teachings and on occasion nationalistic interpretations and political abuse of facts, which is no new phenomenon. The guidance of Professor David Bates, President of Battle and District Historical Society, has been invaluable.

In terms of the period covered this book, it is the 'first' of a trilogy from Battle and District Historical Society covering the history of Battle and eastern Sussex between the dawn of time and the Dissolution of Battle Abbey in 1538, via the not inconsequential year 1066, based on material from its writings and archives and considerable further exploration. The 'second' book in the series was first published in 2015 and minimally revised in 2018. Co-written by the author and his colleague Neil Clephane-Cameron it is titled *1066 and the Battle of Hastings – Preludes, Events and Postscripts*. It considered why William of Normandy's invasion occurred, the events of 1066 itself and its immediate aftermath. Some relevant parts of the early prelude content of that book have necessarily been re-used, reviewed, revised and added to in this book. Work from this book will inevitably need to be worked into any 2nd edition of that book! The 'third' book written by the author is *Conquest to Dissolution* which was published in 2019 and again covered eastern Sussex, but from 1067 to 1538. This, which is in time terms the last book of the trilogy, covered a period for which more and more information becomes available as the years advance, with much richer sources.

Also, for BDHS Neil Clephane-Cameron has produced a second edition of a small book, *The 1066 Malfosse Walk,* which discusses the possible sites for the Malfosse incident at the end of the Battle of Hastings and provides the route for a guided walk. Taking a big jump forward in time George Kiloh's book, *The Brave Remembered – Battle at War 1914–1919,* covered the first world war (published 2015). George is working at the time of writing on another book about Battle between 1830–1870, a time of considerable changes, a veritable time of 'Rural Revolution', and a further book about significant of Battle and district. More volumes by other authors, covering later periods, are in preparation to fill the 1538 to 1980 gap, and in 2017 Adrian and Sarah Hall wrote an intriguing monograph, *Edmund Langdon and his World*, about a 1610 resident of Battle claiming to be a 'General practitioner in Astronomie and Physicke'.

It is unlikely that BDHS will produce a book covering the ownership of Battle Abbey from 1721 until it passed into public ownership in 1976 as that has been very ably covered in Roy Pryce's excellent self-published book, *Battle Abbey and the Websters – Two Hundred Years of Ambition Profligacy and Misfortune*, published in 2005. But we are interested in researching and writing more about the people and lay events of the town and villages of Battle and District after 1538 until 1830, after 1870, and of the 1538–1721 history of the Abbey and its noble owners. Some of BDHS's on-line articles in Collectanea concern these times in eastern Sussex.

Other books by BDHS members, but not published by BDHS, include Braybrook's in depth *A History of the Parish Church of Battle* in 2009, Foord's *Battle Abbey and Battle Churches since 1066* in 2011, with a follow-up book *The Methodist Road to Battle* in 2013 which explored how Methodism had come to eastern Sussex via an interesting 'two-pronged' route, one involving John Wesley and the second via militia from the north of England. *Battle at War 1939–45* published by Battle Museum of Local History in 2019 was edited by Adrian and Sarah Hall and described life in Battle during WW2 with some stories of local WW2 heroes, and *The Battle Tapestry* self-published in 2019 by Christina Greene, is the story of the designing and making of an embroidery in 'Bayeux' style which is a visual history of Battle from 1066 to 1115. David and Barbara Martin have researched and written about much of the local built environment from the early medieval period including, in 2016, *Building Battle Town: an Architectural History, 1066–1750* co-authored with Christopher Whittick and Jane Brisco .

In terms of other 'recent' local history books for the wider eastern Sussex, much has been written about Rye: Leopold Vidler's *A New History of Rye*, Graham Mayhew's *Tudor Rye* and Gillian Draper's *Rye – A History of a Sussex Cinque Port to 1660*, and for Winchelsea there are *Winchelsea – A Tale of a Medieval Town* and *Winchelsea – a Port of Stranded Pride* both by Malcolm Pratt. Other local histories include *Twenty Centuries in Sedlescombe* by Beryl Lucy, *Brede – a Story of a Sussex Parish* by Edmund Austen and

Pevensey the Port and the Levels by G C Sacret, *Making History in Pevensey* by Alan Starr, and *Historic Hastings* by J Mainwaring Baines. Only a few pages of any of these refer to the pre-1066 era.

The *Sussex Archaeological Collections*, published regularly by The Sussex Archaeological Society, are a deep well of local historical knowledge as are the publications of the Sussex Record Society and the Wealden Iron Research Group. HAARG produce a regular informative journal but unfortunately have not published them online, although copies are available on request. Numbers of small books about specific subjects have been produced by other local historical groups, but no one has yet written a comprehensive follow up to Baines' book about Hastings. It would be a large task, but a rewarding one.

A lot of history, including local history, is available on the internet, some very good indeed, some very bad: mischievously bad and erroneous. Even the best is vulnerable to extinction if the websites are closed without ensuring their archiving. Fortunately, the British Library is alert to this, and the Open UK Web Archive is a collection of selected websites archived by the British Library and its partners since 2004. Selected websites continue to be added to this open access collection. Anyone can nominate a UK website for inclusion, as long it has a .uk or other UK geographic top-level domain such as .scot or .cymru and are published in the UK, but of course the recommendation may not be accepted. The simple message is archive it or lose it.

One standout item that that the author has learnt from writing about history is summed up by Cunliffe below. How history is written about is changing all the time, as new ways of exploring history and more accurately dating history emerge. And its understanding is indeed affected by our social, educational and political environment, and the point in time during which the work is being formulated.

What I knew yesterday has been supplanted by what I know today, a lot of healthy scepticism, a dose of lateral thinking... and the occasional bit of 'flexible logic'.'

The author

... our views of the past will always be conditioned by current preconceptions: our understanding is circumscribed by our being.

Sir Barry Cunliffe

Appendix

This solely concerns the names of TRE land holders and overlords. The data is from *Domesday*, listed by hundred and manor, estate or vill, with values of each holding, and numbers of churches, mills, salterns and burgesses.

Information is mainly from the *PASE* database, supplemented from Phillimore's *Domesday Book of Sussex*, from which the entry number and additional detail is taken. Some additional information around Pevensey/Eastbourne is suggested from a supposed Charter of Fécamp Abbey dated 1054

Lordships of land by the Godwin family are blocked in yellow, by King Edward and his sister Countess Goda in purple and by the Church in blue. Wilton Abbey was at this time under the patronage of Edith, wife of Edward the Confessor. Vill names in red indicate that they cannot be accurately located within the hundred on modern mapping. *Innominate* means that the name of the vill is unknown. Some Pevensey controlled vills lay in Hastings hundreds.

Note: values are given as pounds, shillings and pence (£ s d). Until 1971 there were 20 shillings (s) in £1 and 12 pence(d) in each shilling. A simple rounded conversion is to multiply the number of shillings by 5 to convert to modern pence (p)… and add half the d's to the nearest lower p if under 6d and the nearest higher p if over 6p.

Hundred and Vill	No	TRE Holder	TRE Lordship	PASE info & no. Phillimore data if no PASE entry	TRE Value £ s d	Churches	Mills	Salterns	Burgesses
Ninfield									
Hooe	9.1		**Earl Godwine**	Earl Godwine [Godwine 51] held 12 hides (also see 10.77)	£25	1	1	30	
Catsfield	9.2	Ælfhelm	**King Edward**	Ælfhelm [Ælfhelm 29] held 1.50 hides. His/her lord was King Edward (15)			1	1	
Medehei	9.3	Osweard	**King Edward**	Osweard [Osweard 12] held 3 virgates.	£4			5	
Ninfield	9.4	Blæc	**King Edward**	Blæc [Blæc 1] held 3 hides	£6	1			

Hundred and Vill	No	TRE Holder	TRE Lordship	PASE info & no. Phillimore data if no PASE entry	TRE Value £ s d	Churches	Mills	Salterns	Burgesses
Foxearle									
Herste... (monceux)	9.5		Eadmer, possibly of Fécamp	Eadmær, priest [Eadmær 15] held 5 hides. Must be the same priest as at Pevensey (10.1)	£6	1			
Wartling	9.6	Alnoth	King Edward	Earl Alnoth [Alnoth 4] held 5 hides. His/her lord was King Edward [Edward 15]	£10			3	
Ashburn-ham	9.7	Siward	King Edward	Siward [Siward 2] held 2.5 hides. His/her lord was King Edward [Edward 15]	£6	1		3	
Frankwell *in Ash-burnham*	9.8	Northman	?	Northmann [Northmann 1] held 1.5 hides	£2				
Innominate	9.9		Two free men	Phillimore: 1hide	£1 10s				
Innominate	9.33		King Edward	Phillimore: 1.5 virgates. Possibly adjacent to **9,32**	£2				
Innominate	9.1	Hernetoc	?	Hernetoc [Hernetoc 1] held 1 virgate	10s				
Bexhill									
Bexhill	9.11		Bishop Æthelric	Æthelric Bishop of Selsey [Æthelric 50] held 20 hides.	£20	1			
Bexhill	9.11		Bishop Æthelric	Æthelric Bishop of Selsey [Æthelric 50] held 1/2 hide		1			
Innominate	9.12	?	?	Phillimore : 2 virgates	8s				

Hundred and Vill	No	TRE Holder	TRE Lordship	PASE info & no. Phillimore data if no PASE entry	TRE Value £ s d	Churches	Mills	Salterns	Burgesses
Bullington *in Bexhill*	9.13	Leonoth	**King Edward**	Leofnoth [Leofnoth 9] held 5. His/her lord was King Edward [Edward 15].	£6				20*
Baldslow									
Filsham	9.14		**King Edward**	King Edward [Edward 15] held 15 hides.	£14				
Filsham *church*	9.14	Wulfmær	**King Edward**	Wulfmær [Wulfmær 31] held 1 virgate in Filsham (church, St Ethelburgas?). His/her lord was King Edward [Edward 15]	5s	1			
Hollington	9.15		**Godwin and Alstan**	Godwine [Godwine 84] held 2.25 hides. Alstan [Alstan 1] held 2.25 hides.	15s				
Cortesley in Hollington	9.16		**Goldwine**	Goldwine [Goldwine 1] held 6 hides. Also, Goldwine [Goldwine 1] held another 4.5 hides (Unvalued).	£5				
Westfield	9.17		**Wynstan**	Wynstan [Wynstan 1] held 1 hide, 2 virgates	£1				
Crowhurst	9.18		**Earl Harold**	Earl Harold [Harold 3] held 6 hides	£8				
Wilting	9.19		**Two free men**	2 free men held 4 hides	£5				
Innominate	9.2		**Two free men**	Phillimore: 3 virgates	£0				

* were these from Hastings after the Conquest

Hundred and Vill	No	TRE Holder	TRE Lordship	PASE info & no. Phillimore data if no PASE entry	TRE Value £ s d	Churches	Mills	Salterns	Burgesses
Luet or Ivet (Lidham)	9.113		Leofric	Leofric [Leofric 79] held 1 virgate	3s				
Claverham	9.114		Osweard	Osweard [Osweard 12] held 2 virgates (in Pevensey Rape)	5s				
Hailesaltede									
Whatlington	9.21		Earl Harold	Earl Harold [Harold 3] held 0.50 hides	£2 10s				
Mountfield	9.22	Goda	King Edward	Goda [Goda 16] held 1 hide. His/her lord was King Edward [Edward 15].	£3				
Innominate	9.24		Alnoth	Alnoth [Alnoth 4] held 1.50 hides	£2 10s				
Netherfield	9.23	Goda	King Edward	Goda [Goda 16] held 1.50 hides	£2 10s			8	
Uckham	8.3	Wulfbeald	Earl Godwine	Wulfbeald [Wulfbeald 1] held 0.50 hides. His/her lord was Earl Godwine [Godwine 51].	£1				
Beech	9.25		Wulfbeald	Wulfbeald [Wulfbeald 1] held 1 virgate.	2s				
Broohham near Catsfield	9.26		Edith	Edith (Eddid) not in PASE, Phillimore says 1/2 hide	£1				
Eyelids	9.27	Leofwine	Earl Leofwine	Leofwine [Leofwine 102] held 1 virgate. His/her lord was Earl Leofwine [Leofwine 69]	5s				
Chalvington	9.115		?	In Pevensey Rape					

Hundred and Vill	No	TRE Holder	TRE Lordship	PASE info & no. Phillimore data if no PASE entry	TRE Value £ s d	Churches	Mills	Salterns	Burgesses
Heighton *in Beckley*	**9.116** **9.117** **9.118**		Godwine	Godwine [Godwine 84] held 2 virgates worth 4s. Plus, Godwine [Godwine 84] held 1 virgate worth 2s. Plus, Godwine [Godwine 84] held 1 virgate worth 2s? Not duplicates, must have been grouped separate holdings	8s				
Brightling	**9.31**	Two brothers	King Edward	Phillimore: 1 hide	£5 10s	1			
Dallington	**9.32**		Northman	Northmann [Northmann 1] held 1 hide	?				
Innominate	**9.119**		A free man	Phillimore: 1 virgate	15d				
Warbleton	**9.34**		Countess Goda	Gode [Gode 6] held 1 hide.	40s				
Via Pevensey	Ex VCH		Multiple names	Freemen held estates to total value	£2 10s				
Via Pevensey	Ex VCH		Wilton Abbey	Ecclesiastical holdings mainly Wilton Abbey. Estates to total value	£2 2s 6d				
Via Pevensey	Ex VCH		Mainly Countess Goda	Royal estates to total value	£10 11s				
Via Pevensey	Ex VCH		Godwin family	Godwin estates to total value	£2 8s				
Shoyswell									
Via Pevensey	Ex VCH		Multiple names	Freemen held estates to total value	£2 13s 4d				

Hundred and Vill	No	TRE Holder	TRE Lordship	PASE info & no. Phillimore data if no PASE entry	TRE Value £ s d	Churches	Mills	Salterns	Burgesses
Via Pevensey	Ex VCH		Wilton Abbey	Ecclesiastical holdings mainly by Wilton Abbey. Estates to total value	£4 3s				
Via Pevensey	Ex VCH		Edward and Goda	Royal estates to total value	£3 18s				
Via Pevensey	Ex VCH		Godwin	Godwin estates to total value	£1				
Hazelhurst	9.6	Bishop Æthelric	King Edward	Æthelric Bishop of Selsey [Æthelric 50] held 4.50 hides.	£5 14s	1			
Henhurst									
Salehurst	9.82		Countess Goda	Gode [Gode 6] held 0.50 hide.	£1	1			
Drigsel in Salehurst	9.83	Cana		Cana [Cana 1] held 3.50 hides, 1 virgate	£3				
Innominate		Cana		Cana [Cana 1] held 1 hide	£1 10s				
Innominate		Leofgifu		Leofgifu [Leofgifu 4] held 0.50 hide	£1				
Innominate		Northman		Northmann [Northmann 1] held 0.50 hides	£1				
Innominate		Azur		Azur [Azur 1] held 1 virgate	10s				
Via Pevensey	Ex VCH		Multiple names	Freemen held estates to total value	£1 18s				
Via Pevensey	Ex VCH		Wilton Abbey	Ecclesiastical holding by Wilton Abbey,	5s				
Via Pevensey	Ex VCH		Mainly Goda	Royal estates to total value	£8 2s				
Babinrerode									
Kitchenham	9.103		Eadric	Eadric [Eadric 84] held 0.50 hides	10s				

Hundred and Vill	No	TRE Holder	TRE Lordship	PASE info & no. Phillimore data if no PASE entry	TRE Value £ s d	Churches	Mills	Salterns	Burgesses
Udimore	9.104	Algar	**Earl Godwine**	Algar [Algar 4] held 6 hides. His/her lord was Earl Godwine [Godwine 51]	£8	1			
Guestling									
Guestling	9.105	Wulfbeald/ Ulbald	**King Edward**	Wulfbeald [Wulfbeald 1] held 4.50 hides. His/her lord was King Edward [Edward 15].	£5				
Ivet (Lidham)	9.106	Leofræd	**Earl Godwine**	Leofræd [Leofræd 1] held 1 hide. His/ her lord was Earl Godwine [Godwine 51]	?				
Fairlight	9.107	Wulfmær	**Earl Godwine**	Wulfmær [Wulfmær 31] held 6 hides. His/her lord was Earl Godwine [Godwine 51]	£5	1			
Rameslie	5.1		**Fécamp Abbey**	Phillimore: 20 hides. See Sawyer: S949 (1017/1032) and S 982 (1028/1035). Confirmed by Harthacnut 1040/1042	£34	5		100	64
Rameslie (Hastings)	5.1		**Fécamp Abbey**	As above. There is no mention of Brede etc					4
Goldspur									
Evebentone	9.108		**Earl Godwine**	Earl Godwine [Godwine 51] held 0.50 hide	12s				

Hundred and Vill	No	TRE Holder	TRE Lordship	PASE info & no. Phillimore data if no PASE entry	TRE Value £ s d	Churches	Mills	Salterns	Burgesses
Playden	9.109	Sigewulf	King Edward	Sigewulf [Sigewulf 13] held 4 hides. His/her lord was King Edward [Edward 15] (£6)	£6				
Playden	9.109		Sigewulf	Sigewulf [Sigewulf 13] held 1 hide (no value given).	?	1			
Iden	9.11		Eadnoth	Eadnoth [Eadnoth 27] held 3 virgates	£1 10s				
Glossams in Beckley	9.111		Three men	Phillimore: 1 1/2 hides	£2				
Innominate	9.112		Edward	Edward [Edward 34] held 1 virgate	5s				
Staple									
Ewhurst	9.12	Ælfhere	King Edward	Ælfhere [Ælfhere 28] held 6 hides. His/her lord was King Edward [Edward 15]	£10				
Bodiam in Ewhurst	9.12			As above as one manor, but the manor Hall was here					
Highham (Northiam)	9.121		Earl Godwine	Earl Godwine [Godwine 51] held 2.50 hides.	£5				
Sedlescombe	9.122	Leofsige	Countess Goda	Leofsige [Leofsige 45] held 1 hide, 3 virgates. His/her lord was Gode [Gode 6].	£3	1			
Lordine	9.123	Wynstan	Osweard	Wynstan [Wynstan 1] held 0.50 hide. His/her lord was Osweard [Osweard 12].	14s				

Hundred and Vill	No	TRE Holder	TRE Lordship	PASE info & no. Phillimore data if no PASE entry	TRE Value £ s d	Churches	Mills	Salterns	Burgesses
Bellhurst	9.124		Ealdred	Ealdræd [Ealdræd 1] held 2 virgates	7s				
Innominate	9.125		?	Phillimore: 3 acres	10s				
Innominate	9.126		?	Phillimore: 1/2 hide	?				
Innominate	9.127		?	Phillimore: 1 virgate	5s				
Footland	9.128		Wynstan	Wynstan [Wynstan 1] held 0.50 hide	?				
Hurst	9.129		Wulfwyn	Phillimore 1/2 hide	10s				
Wellhead in Ewhurst	9.13		Four brothers	Phillimore: 1 hide and a hall	£3 6s				
Basingeham	9.13		Ælfgeat	Ælfgeat [Ælfgeat 10] held 2 virgates in Bassingham, Sussex TRE.	?				
Innominate belong to Eyelid	9.29		Earl Leofwine	Phillimore: Land for 1 plough, 1 villager	4s				
Innominate belong to Eyelid	9.28		Earl Leofwine	Earl Leofwine [Leofwine 69] held 2 virgates	?				
Innominate	9.3		Cana	Cana [Cana 1] held 1 virgate.	4s				
Borough of Pevensey									
	10.1		King Edward		£3 16s 9d	1			24

There was also a neighbouring large hundred of Willingdon which is not included in this study as it was a 'Downland' hundred outwith of and relatively uninfluencing the 'Wealden' area.

Hundred and Vill	No	TRE Holder	TRE Lordship	PASE info & no. Phillimore data if no PASE entry	TRE Value £ s d	Churches	Mills	Salterns	Burgesses
	10.1		**Bishop of Selsey**	Aethelric II of Selsey, was deposed after 1066 and Bishop Stigand appears by 1070. He moved the diocese to Chichester in 1075. He fell out with King William and lost lands					15
	10.1		**Possibly Fécamp**	Eadmer a priest					15
	10.1		**Possibly Fécamp**	Ordemer a priest				?	5
	10.1		**Possibly Fécamp**	Doda a priest					3
Eastbourne									
Eastbourne	9.88 9.90 10.2		**King Edward**	King Edward [Edward 15] held 1 hide value 20s., 0.50 hides value 20s., 46 hides value £95 5s., plus 1 hide value unknown	£97 5s	1*	1	16	
Hankham	10.82		**King Edward**	Phillimore 1 hide and 1/2 virgate, part of Eastbourne	9s				
Hankham	10.81		?	Phillimore 2 hides, part of Eastbourne	15s				
Dill									
Pengest	10.5	Wulfgeat	**King Edward**	Wulfgeat [Wulfgeat 20] held 1 virgate. His/her lord was King Edward [Edward 15]	?				

*given to Fécamp Abbey in 1054

Hundred and Vill	No	TRE Holder	TRE Lordship	PASE info & no. Phillimore data if no PASE entry	TRE Value £ s d	Churches	Mills	Salterns	Burgesses
Hawkridge *in Hellingly*	10.51		Brictwy	Phillimore: 1/2 hide, plus another 1/2 hide in Hastings Rape	£1				
Hendon *in Hailsham*	10.52		Almær	Phillimore: 1/2 hide	9s				
Pevensey									
Wooton	10.67		Six thegns	Phillimore: Land for 5 ploughs, mill, salterns	£1 10s		1	5	
Hailsham	10.68		Alnoth	Alnoth [Alnoth 4] held 1.50 hides	110s			13	
Chenonolle	10.69		Toki	Toki [Toki 10] held 2 hides	£2				
Willingdon (Willingdon holdings may be outliers of Willingdon Hundred lying within Pevensey Hundred)	9.96 / 9.101		Goda (a free man)	Goda [Goda 16] held 1.50 virgates in value 10s. / Goda [Goda 16] held 0.50 hides worth 20s.	£1 10s				
Willingdon	9.45 9.67 9.7		Countess Goda	Gode [Gode 6] held 1.50 virgates worth 5s . Gode [Gode 6] held 0.50 virgates (Phill: 1s). Gode [Gode 6] held 0.50 hides worth 40s	£2 6s				
Willingdon	9.46		Wulfmaer	Wulfmær [Wulfmær 31] held 1 virgate	3s				
Willingdon	10.7		Leofweard	Leofweard [Leofweard 4] held 1.50 hides	10s			11	
Cudnor in Westham	10.72		Beorth-wine	Beorhtwine [Beorhtwine 21] held 1 hide	?				

Hundred and Vill	No	TRE Holder	TRE Lordship	PASE info & no. Phillimore data if no PASE entry	TRE Value £ s d	Churches	Mills	Salterns	Burgesses
Cudnor in Westham	10.72		Beorth-wine	Beorhtwine [Beorhtwine 21] held 1 hide	?				
Horsey	10.73	Clerks in common	Alms of St Michael	2 hides. Was this some land given to Fécamp Abbey in 1054?	10s				
Horns	10.76		?	1 hide	13s				
Horns	10.75		Three men	2 hides	£1 5s				
Renching in Westham	10.78		Two free men	2 hides	16s				
Peelings part of Hankham	10.79		Alweard and Algar	Alweard [Alweard 2] held 2 hides. Algar [Algar 4] held 2 hides. As two manors	?				
Peelings part of Hankham	10.71		?	?	3s				
Langley	10.8		Leofmær, Bricstan, Alfheah	Phillimore: 1 hide to each of Leofmær and Bricstan, plus 1 hide to Alfheah	16s 8d				
Bowley in Hailsham	10.83		Earl Harold	Earl Harold [Harold 3] held 0.50 hides	15s			4	
Bowley in Hailsham	10.84		?Earl Harold	0.5 hide (Eastbourne lands)	9s				
Hooe Level	10.77		Earl Godwine	Earl Godwine [Godwine 51] held 2 virgates in Hooe. See 9.1 above, with which value probably shared	?			4	
Wooton	10.85		? Earl Harold	The entry looks like a 'lost' side note concerning where 13s should go	13s				

Cover Image

The cover image is derived from the 'Franks Casket', found by Sir Augustus Franks in an antique shop in Paris in 1857, and donated in 1867 to the British Museum. The whalebone casket is of Anglo-Saxon origin and dated about 700ce. It is carved with both Christian and pagan scenes, in an odd mixture of Roman, Germanic and Christian traditions. It has eleven inscriptions mostly in runic, apart from three words in Latin text.

It was made at the time of significant religious changes in Anglo-Saxon culture. Linguistic evidence suggests that it may have been made in Northumbria, but as the casket lacks Celtic symbolism and the dress style of the figures is Germanic an eastern English origin further to the south is possible. It is unknown how the casket ended up in Paris.

The small area chosen for the cover illustration is from the lower right of the front panel of the casket and depicts two of the three magi presenting gifts to Mary and the new-born Jesus.

Bibliographies

I love to lose myself in other men's minds. When I am not walking, I am reading: I cannot sit and think. Books think for me.

Charles Lamb

Abels, R. 'English Logistics and military administration, 871–1066: The Impact of the Viking Wars', in Jorgensen AN and Clausen, BL (eds): Papers from an international research seminar at the Danish National Museum, Copenhagen, 2–4 May 1996: *Military aspects of Scandinavian society in a European perspective, AD 1–1300,* (1997)

Aldiss, DT. et al. *National Geological Screening: The Wealden district. British Geological Survey Commissioned Report,* CR/17/099, (2018)

Anonymous *Vita Edwardi Regis* British Library Harley MS 526 (for a translation see Luard below)

Anscombe, A. 'The Pedigree of Godwine' *Transactions of the Royal Historical Society,* 37, (1913): 129–50

Baines, JM. *Historic Hastings* (1955)

Barker, E. 'Sussex Anglo-Saxon Charters, part I' *Sussex Archæological Collections (SAC)*; 86, (1947): 42–101

Barker, E. 'Sussex Anglo-Saxon Charters, part II' *SAC,* 87, (1948): 112–163

Barlow, F. *Edward the Confessor,* (1997)

Barlow, F. *The Godwins: The Rise and Fall of a Noble Dynasty,* (2002)

Barlow, LW. 'The Antecedents of Earl Godwine of Wessex', *New England Historical and Genealogical Register,* lxi, (1957)

Barral i Altet, X. and Bates, D. *La Tapisserie de Bayeux,* (2019)

Bates, D. (ed.) *1066 in Perspective,* (2018)

Bates, D. *Normandy Before 1066,* (1982)

Bates, D. *William the Conqueror,* (2016)

Baxter, S. 'Edward the Confessor and the Succession Question', in R. Mortimer, (ed.), *Edward the Confessor: The Man & the Legend,* (2009)

Berry, BJL. *Hastingleigh, 1000–2000AD,* (2002)

Blair, PH. *Roman Britain and Early England, 55BC–AD871.* (1975)

Bloch, RH. 'Animal Fables, the Bayeux Tapestry and the making of the Anglo-Norman World', *Poetica,* vol. 37, no. 3/4, (2005): 285–309

Bloche, M.. *Le chartrier de l'abbaye de la Trinité de Fécamp : étude et édition critique,*

928/929–1190; postérité du fonds, [Doctoral thesis], Normandie Université, (2019)

Bolton, T. *'The Empire of Cnut the Great: Conquest and the Consolidation of Power'* in *Northern Europe in the Early Eleventh Century*. (2009)

Bosanquet, G (Trans.) *Eadmer's History of Recent Events in England: 'Historia Novorum in Anglia'*", (1964)

Bowden, M, A. Brodie, & F. Small, 'Pevensey Castle, Pevensey, East Sussex: architectural, archae-ological and aerial investigation', *Historic England Research Report* Series no. 39/2019

Brandon, P. (ed.), *The South Saxons,* (1978)

Brodribb, G. and H. Cleere, 'The Classis Britannica Bath-house at Beauport Park, East Sussex', *Britannia,* 19, 1988

Brookes, S. & S. Harrington, *The Kingdom and People of Kent,* AD400–1066: *Their History and Archaeology,* (2010).

Brooks, N. *Anglo-Saxon Myths: State and Church, 400–1066,* (1998)

Brooks, NP. 'The unidentified forts of the Burghal Hidage', *Medieval Archaeology,* 7, 1964

Bruce, JC. *The Bayeux Tapestry Elucidated* (1856) via http://www.gutenberg.org

Butler, M. *The Burghal Hidage – A Text of the 'A' Version,* (2014)

Campbell, A. (ed.) *'Encomium Emmae Reginae',* Royal Historical Society, Camden Third Series Vol. LXXII, (1949)

Campbell, A. (ed.), *The Chronicle of Æthelweard,* (1962)

Campbell, J. (ed.), *The Anglo-Saxons,* (1982)

Champness, C. 'Bexhill to Hasting Link Road 2013', *Archaeological and Geoarchaeological Evaluation Report,* (2013)

Chefneux, H. 'Les fables dans la tapissserie de Bayeux', *Romania* Vol. LX (1934): 1–35

Chevalier, CT. 'The Frankish origin of the Hastings tribe', *SAC,* Vol. 104: 56–62

Cinque Ports Chronicle, 4, No. 71, (1840)

Cleeve, J and Williams, R. 'Cliff Erosion in East Sussex', *Sussex Studies,* No.5. 1987

Coates, R. 'On the alleged Frankish origin of the Hastings tribe', *SAC,* Vol. 117: 263–264

Cohen, KM., PL. Gibbard, & HJT. Weerta. 'North Sea palaeogeographical reconstructions for the last one million years', *Netherlands Journal of Geosciences,* Vol. 93, 7–29

Colgrave, B. (ed./trans.). *The Life of Bishop Wilfred by Eddius Stephanus,* (1927)

Collier, JS. *et al.* 'Streamlined islands and the English Channel megaflood hypothesis', *Global and Planetary Change Volume,* 135, December 2015, 190–206

Combes P. & M. Lyne 'Hastings, Haestingceastre and Hastingaport' *SAC,* Vol. 133: 213–24

Cook, AS. (ed.). *Asser's Life of Alfred,* (1905)

Cornwell, K and L. Cornwell. 'Hastings Country Park Hidden Landscape Project', *HAARG Journal New Series,* 39, Special Issue (2019)

Cornwell, K. and Cornwell, L. 'Roman Coins from the HAARG Area'. *HAARG Journal New Series,* 27, 2009: 8–11

Cowdrey, HEJ. 'Towards an Interpretation of the Bayeux Tapestry', *Anglo-Norman Studies,* X (1987), Proceedings of the Battle Conference

Crouch, D. *The Normans: The History of a Dynasty,* 2006

CRS. *The Numismatic Chronicle,* Vol 3 (Jul 1840–Jan 1841): 65–67

Cunliffe, B. *Britain Begins,* (2012)

Curwen, EC. *Archaeology of Sussex,* (1954)

Darby, HC. & Campbell, EMJ. (eds.) *The Domesday Geography of South-East England,* (1971)

Darlington, RR. (ed.), P. McGurk (ed. & trans.), Bray J. (trans.). *The Chronicle of John of Worcester: Volume II: The Annals from 450–1066,* (1995)

Davison, BK. 'The Burghal Hidage fort of Eorpeburnan: a suggested identification', *Medieval Archaeology,* Vol. 16 1972: 123–7

Dickinson, A. 'Playden or Saltcote: Rye's troublesome neighbour', *The Newsletter of the Romney Marsh Research Trust,* (Spring 2010)

Douglas, DC. *William the Conqueror,* (1964)

Drewett, P., D. Rudling, and M. Gardiner, *The South East to AD1000,* (1988)

Eddison, J., M. Gardiner, and A. Long, (eds.). 'Romney Marsh: Environmental Change and Human Occupation in a Coastal Lowland', *OUCA Monograph,* 46 (1998)

Elliott, S. *Sea Eagles of Empire: The Classis Britannica and the Battles for Britain,* (2016)

Ellis, PB. *Caesar's Invasion of Britain,* (1978)

Evans, J. *The ancient bronze implements, weapons and ornaments of Great Britain and Ireland,* (1881)

Faith, R. *The English Peasantry and the Growth of Lordship,* (1999)

Fields, N. *Rome's Saxon Shore – Coastal Defences of Britain AD250–500,* (2006)

Fisher, DJV. *The Anglo-Saxon Age,* (1973)

Fleming, R. *Britain after Rome – The Fall and Rise 400 to 1070,* (2010)

Fleming, R. *Kings and Lords in Conquest England,* (2008)

Foord, K. 'R4.2a A Critique and Comparison of "Companion Rolls of the Conquest", some known as 'Battle Abbey Rolls', and Foord, K. 'R4.2b Data underlying the "Companion Rolls of the Conquest" – paper R4.2a': from http://battlehistory. btck.co.uk/Collectanea-OurVirtualLibrary/RGrey

Foord, K. & N. Clephane-Cameron, *1066 and the Battle of Hastings, Preludes, Events and Postscripts.* (2015 – reprinted 2016 and 2018)

Foord, KD. 'The Rapes of Sussex, Hundreds of Hastings Rape and the people of the Rape of Hastings to 1538', Article A2.5 in http://battlehistory.btck.co.uk/ Collectanea-OurVirtualLibrary/ABlack

Forester, T (trans.) *The Ecclesiastical History of England and Normandy by Ordericus Vitali,* Vol.1. (1853)

Fradley, M. & S. Newsome, 'East Hill, Hastings, East Sussex : A landscape survey and investigation', *English Heritage Research Department Report Series,* No. 35–2008

Frere, SS. *Britannia, a History of Roman Britain,* (1978)

Fuller, T. ed. by JS Brewer, *The Church History of Britain, from the Birth of Jesus Christ until the Year MDCXLVIII,* (1845)

Gade, KE. 'Northern Light on the Battle of Hastings', *Viator,* Vol 28, (1997): 65

Gardiner, M. 'Economy and Landscape Change in Post-Roman and early Medieval Sussex 450–1175' in D. Rudling (ed.) *The Archaeology of Sussex to AD2000.*

Gardiner, M. *Medieval settlement and society in the eastern High Weald,* Ph.D. thesis (1995)

Gardiner, M. 'Some Lost Anglo-Saxon Charters and the endowment of Hastings College', *SAC* Vol. 127, (1989): 39–48

Gelling, M. *Place-Names in the Landscape,* (1985).

Gibbard, P. 'How Britain became an island', *Nature Precedings,* 10.1038/ npre.2007.12.05.1.1 (2007)

Giles, JA. (ed.). 'Gildas: 'The Works of Gildas' in *Six Old English Chronicles,* (1866)

Giles, JA. (ed.). 'Nennius: History of the Britons' in *Six Old English Chronicles,* (1866).

Giles, JA. (ed.). 'Chronicle of Æthelweard' in *Old English Chronicles,* (1906)

Giles, JA. *William of Malmesbury's Chronicle of the Kings of England,* (1847)

Gordon, E. 'The site of Eynsham Abbey: a Historical Note' in Grey, M. and N. Clayton, 'Excavations on the site of Eynsham Abbey, 1971', *Oxoniensia,* XIII (1978)

Grainge, C. and G. Grainge, 'The Pevensey Expedition: Brilliantly executed plan or near disaster?' in Morillo, S. (ed.) *The Battle of Hastings,* (1996): 129–142

Green, T. *Britons and Anglo-Saxons: Lincolnshire AD400–650,* (2012)

Greene, C. *The Battle Tapestry,* (2019)

Grierson, P. 'A Visit of Earl Harold to Flanders in 1056', *The English Historical Review,* Vol. 51, No. 201, (1936): 90–97

Grose, F. *A Treatise on Ancient Armour and Weapons,* Plate 13, (1784)

Gupta, S. *et al.* 'Catastrophic flooding origin of shelf valley systems in the English Channel', *Nature,* 448, (19 July 2007): 342–5

Hariulf, M. (Lot, F. ed.). *Chronique de Saint Riquier,* (1894/2010)

Härke, H. 'Anglo-Saxon immigration and ethnogenesis', *Medieval Archaeology,* Vol 55 (2011): 1–28

Harmer, FE. *Anglo-Saxon Writs,* (1952)

Harris, RB. *Pevensey: Historic Character Assessment Report,* (2008)

Harris, RB. *Summary of historic settlement development in the High Weald,* (2011)

Harris, RB. *The making of the High Weald,* (2003)

Haskins, CH. 'A Charter of Cnut for Fécamp', *English Historical Review,* 33, (1918): 342–44

Haslam, J. 'King Alfred and the Vikings: Strategies and Tactics 876 to 886AD' in Semple, S. (ed.), *Saxon Studies in Archaeology and History,* Vol 13, (2005)

Hawkes, C. & GC. Dunning. 'The Belgae of Gaul and Britain', *Archaeological Journal,*

Vol. 87 (1930): 150–335 [Published online: 18 Jul 2014]

Hicks, C. and S. Lemagnen. *The Bayeux Tapestry,* (2016)

Higham, NJ. (ed.). *Britons in Anglo-Saxon England,* (2007)

Higham, NJ. 'From sub-Roman Britain to Anglo-Saxon England: Debating the Insular Dark Ages', *History Compass,* 2, (2004): 1–29

Higham, NJ. and Ryan, MJ. *Place-names, Language and the Anglo-Saxon Landscape,* (2011)

Hill, D. *An Atlas of Anglo-Saxon England.* (1981)

Hill, DH. 'The Burghal Hidage – the establishment of a text,' *Medieval Archaeology,* XIII, (1969)

Hooper, N. 'The Housecarls in England in the Eleventh Century.' in Strickland, M. (ed.), *Anglo-Norman Warfare,* (1992)

Howarth, D. *1066: The Year of the Conquest,* 1983

Johnson, S. 'Late Roman defences and the Limes' in Johnston, RDE (ed.), 'Research Report No 18 – The Saxon Shore', *The Council for British Archaeology,* 1977

Joliffe, JEA. 'The Domesday Hidation of Sussex and the Rapes', *The English Historical Review,* Vol. XLV, Issue CLXXIX, (1 July 1930): 427–435

Joliffe, JEA. *Pre-feudal England: the Jutes,* (1962)

Jones, G. 'Communication and Settlement in Ewhurst Parish: the evidence of place names', *Locus Focus forum of the Sussex Place-Names Net,* Vol. 2, No.1, (1998)

Jones, GA. *History of the Vikings,* (1975)

Jones, ME. *The End of Roman Britain,* (1998).

Kelly, SE. *Anglo-Saxon Charters VI: Charters of Selsey,* (1998)

Kelly, SE. 'The Control of Kent in the Ninth Century', *Early Medieval Europe,* 2 (2), (1993): 111–31.

Keynes, S. & M. Lapidge, (trans.), *Asser's Life of King Alfred,* (1983)

King, A. *Strategic Stone Study: A Building Stone Atlas of East Sussex,* Historic England, (2015)

Kirby, DP. *The Earliest English Kings,* (2000).

Laing, L. and J. Laing, *Anglo-Saxon England,* (1979)

Lamb, AW. 'The Belgae of Gaul and Britain: revisiting Cross Channel contacts in the Iron Age', *Studies in Honour of Jan Bouzek,* (2018)

Lapidge, M. (ed.). *The Wiley-Blackwell Encyclopaedia of Anglo-Saxon England.* 2nd edn (2013)

Larson, LM. *Canute the Great,* (1912)

Larson, LM. *The King's Household in England before the Norman Conquest,* (1904)

Lawson, MK. *Cnut – England's Viking King 1016–1035,* (2011)

Le Patourel, J. *The Norman Empire,* (1976)

Leslie K. & Short B. (eds) *An Historical Atlas of Sussex,* (1999)

Leslie, S. *et al.* 'The fine scale genetic structure of the British population', *Nature,* Vol. 519, (2015): 309–314

Licence, T. 'Edward the Confessor and the Succession Question: A Fresh Look at the Sources', *Anglo-Norman Studies 39: Proceedings of the Battle Conference 2016,* (2017)

Licence, T. *Edward the Confessor – Last of the Royal Blood,* (2020)

Lloyd, J. 'The Origin of the Lathes of Kent', *Archaeologia Cantiana,* Vol. 133, (2013)

Loseby, ST. 'Power and Towns in late Roman Britain and Early Anglo-Saxon England' in Ripoll, G. and JM. Gurt, (eds.), *Sedes regiae (ann. 400–800),* (2000): 319–370

Loyn, HR. *The Governance of Anglo-Saxon England 500–1087,* (1984)

Loyn, HR. *The Vikings in Britain,* (1977)

Luard, HR. (ed.) *Lives of Edward the Confessor,*(1858) Available via Internet Archive

Lyne, M. *Excavations at Pevensey Castle 1936 to 1964, British Archaeological Reports,* 503, (2009)

MacWhite, E. 'Irish Bronze Age Trumpets' *Journal of the Royal Society of Antiquaries of Ireland* Vol. 75, No. 2, (1945): 85–106

Mansfield, S. 'The Jute and Saxon settlement of Kent and Sussex', *Battle & District Historical Society Journal,* Vol. 19, (2014)

Margary, ID. *Roman Ways in the Weald,* (1965)

Martin, M. 'Anglo-Saxon Kent', in Williams JH (ed.), *The Archaeology of Kent to AD 800,* (2007)

Mason, E. *The House of Godwine – The History of a Dynasty,* (2004)

Mawer, A. *Problems of Place Name Study,* (1929)

Mawer, A. & FM. Stenton, *The Place Names of Sussex,* (1969)

Mellett, C. *et al.* 'Denudation of the continental shelf between Britain and France at the glacial-interglacial timescale', *Geomorphology,* Vol. 203, (2013): 79–96

Mōmmaerts-Browne, TSM. 'Anglo-Saxon Aristocracy: tracing Lineages', *Foundation for Medieval Genealogy: Foundations,* 1, (6), (2005)

Montigny, Adrien de. *Albums de Croÿ XX,* Comté d'Artois IV, plate 27 – Beaurains Castel, (1610)

Morillo, S. (ed.) *The Battle of Hastings,* (1996): 3–53

Myres, JNL. *The English Settlements,* (1989)

Naismith, R. 'England before 1066' in Bates, D. (ed.) *1066 in Perspective,* (2018)

Nelson, JL. 'Reconstructing a Royal Family: reflections on Alfred, from Asser' in Wood, I. & N. Lund, (eds.). *People and Places in Northern Europe 500–1600: Essays in Honour of Peter Hayes Sawyer,* (1991)

O'Brian, E. *Queen Emma and the Vikings,* (2005)

OpenDomesday: *https://opendomesday.org/*

Oppenheimer, S. *The Origins of the British',* (2007)

Page, W. (ed.). *A History of the County of Sussex: Volume 1,* (1905)

Page, W. (ed.). *A History of the County of Sussex: Volume 2,* (reptd 1973)

Palgrave, F. *The Rise and Progress of the English Commonwealth: Anglo-Saxon Period. Containing the Anglo-Saxon Policy, and the Institutions arising out of Laws and*

Usages which prevailed before the Conquest, Vol. 2, (1832): xliv–lxiv

Parker, AG. *et al.* 'A review of the mid-Holocene elm decline in the British Isles', *Progress in Physical Geography,* Vol 26, (2002): 1–45

Phillips, TR. (ed.) and J. Clark, (trans.). *Renatus, Flavius. The Military Institutions of the Romans (De Re Militari).* (2011)

Pitassi, M. *The Navies of Rome,* (2010)

Porter, J. *Bexhill on Sea: A History,* (2015)

Ramsay, JH. *The Foundations of England,* Vol. 2, (1898)

Ray, JE. & W. Budgen, 'Recent find at Eastbourne' *SAC* ,Vol 58, N&Q, (1916): 190–1

Reaney, PH. 'A Survey of Kent Place Names', *Archaeologia Cantiana,* 73 (1959): 62–74

Rivet, ALF. & C. Smith, *The Place-names of Roman Britain,* (1979)

Roberts, RG. *The Place Names of Sussex,* (1914)

Robertson, AJ. (ed.), *Anglo-Saxon Charters,* (1956)

Rowley, T. *An Archaeological Study of the Bayeux Tapestry,* (2016): 56–59

Rudling D. (ed.). *The Archaeology of Sussex to* AD*2000,* (2003)

Salter, HE. *Eynsham Cartulary,* (1907)

Salway, P. *The Oxford History of England: Roman Britain,* (1981)

Salzman, LF. 'Excavations at Pevensey, 1906–7', *SAC,* 51, (1908): 99–114

Salzman, LF. 'Excavations at Pevensey, 1907–8' *SAC,* 52, (1909): 83–95

Salzman, LF. (Ed.). *Victoria County History of Sussex,* Vol 3, (1935)

Salzman, LF. (Ed.). *Victoria County History of Sussex,* Vol 9, (1937, rptd 1973)

Sawyer, PH. *Anglo-Saxon Charters: an annotated list and bibliography,* (1968)

Scargill-Bird, SR. *Custumals of Battle Abbey in the Reigns of Edward I and Edward II, 1283–1312,* (1887)

Scott, E. *A gazetteer of Roman villas in Britain,* (1993)

Searle, WG. *Onomasticon Anglo-Saxonium: A List of Anglo-Saxon Proper Names from the time of Beda to that of King John,* (1897)

Searle, WG. *Anglo-Saxon Bishops, Kings and Nobles: The Succession of the Bishops and the Pedigrees of the Kings and Nobles,* (1899)

Sellar, AM. (trans.). *Bede's Ecclesiastical History of England,* (1907)

Sherley-Price, L. (trans.). *Bede: A history of the English Church and People,* (1955)

Shillito, AP. & NS. Davies. 'Dinosaur-landscape interactions at a diverse Early Cretaceous tracksite (Lee Ness Sandstone, Ashdown Formation, southern England)', *Palaeogeography, Palaeoclimatology, Palaeoecology,* Vol. 514, (Jan 2019): 593–612

Smyth, C. and Jennings, S. 'Mid-to late Holocene Forest Composition and the effects of Clearances in the Combe Haven Valley, East Sussex'. *SAC,* 126, (1988): 1–20

Stenton, F. *Anglo-Saxon England,* (1971)

Stevens, L. and Gilbert, R. *The Eastbourne Roman Villa,* (2017)

Stevenson, J. (trans.). *Chronicle of Chronicles,* published as *Florence of Worcester: A History of the Kings of England from the Invasion of Julius Cæsar to the Accession of Henry II',*

(1988)

Stevenson, WH. (ed.). *Asser's Life of King Alfred,* (1904 [revised edition 1959])

Stevenson, WH. 'The Old English Charters to St. Denis', *English Historical Review,* VI, (1891)

Straker, E. and Margary, ID. 'Ironworks and Communications in the Weald in Roman Times', *The Geographical Journal,* Vol. 92, No. 1, 55–60 (1938*)*

Sturlason, S. *Heimskringla or Chronicle of the Kings of Norway (c.1179–1241),* https://www.gutenberg.org/files/598/598-h/598-h.htm

Sutton, T. 'The Eastbourne Roman Villa', *SAC,* Vol. 90, (1951–2)

Swanton, M. (trans. and ed.) *The Anglo-Saxon Chronicle,* (2000)

Swanton, M. *The Anglo-Saxon Chronicles,* 1996

Tabor, J. 'An accurate account of a tessellated pavement, bath and other Roman antiquities lately discovered near Eastbourne in Sussex', *Philosophical Transactions (No. 351),* 1717

Talbert, RJA. *Rome's World: The Peutinger Map Reconsidered,* (2010)

Taylor, A. 'Belrem' in Chibnall, M. (ed.) *Anglo-Norman Studies,* XIV, (1991): 1–23

Taylor, AJ. 'Evidence for a pre-Conquest origin for the Chapels in Hastings and Pevensey Castles', in Taylor, AJ (ed.) *Chateau Gaillard III – European Castle Studies,* (1969): 144–151

Thomas G. *Resource Assessment and Research Agenda for the Anglo-Saxon Period, Kent,* (2013)

Thorpe, L. *The Bayeux Tapestry and the Norman Invasion,* 1973

Turner, E. 'Roman remains at Eastbourne' *SAC,* Vol. 16, N&Q (1864): 308–9

Tyler, A. *Romney Marsh and the Western River Valleys: An Archaeological Gazetteer,* The Romney Marsh Research Trust (2011)

Viking Ship Museum in Roskilde at *https://www.vikingeskibsmuseet.dk/en/professions/education/knowledge-of-sailing/sail-and-trim*

Walker, HE. 'Bede and the Gewissae: the Political Evolution of the Heptarchy and its Nomenclature' *Cambridge Historical Journal,* Vol. 12.2 (January 1956): 174–186

Walker, I. *Harold the Last Anglo-Saxon King,* 2000

Ward, EM. 'The Evolution of the Hastings Coastline' *The Geographical Journal,* Vol. 56, No. 2, (1920): 107–120

Welch, MG. *Anglo-Saxon England,* (1992)

Welch, MG. in Brandon, P. (ed.). *The South Saxons: Early Anglo-Saxon Sussex,* (1978)

Williams, A. and GH. Martin (eds.). *Domesday Book – A Complete Translation,* (1992)

Williams, A. '1066 and the English' in Bates, D. (ed.) *1066 in Perspective,* (2018)

Williams, A. *The English and the Norman Conquest,* (1995)

Williams, A. *World Before Domesday: The English Aristocracy 871–1066,* (2011)

Williamson, JA. *The Evolution of England,* (1931)

Wilson, DM. *The Bayeux Tapestry,* (1985)

Wood, I. 'The End of Roman Britain: Continental Evidence and Parallels' in Lapidge

M. & D. Dumville (ed.) *Gildas: New Approaches, (1984)*

Woodbridge-Witney, KP. *The Kingdom of Kent*, (1982).

Woodcock, A. 'Gazetteer of Prehistoric, Roman and Saxon Sites in Romney Marsh and the surrounding area' in J Eddison and C Green (eds). *Romney Marsh: evolution, occupation, reclamation.* Oxford Committee for Archaeology Monograph (1988): 177–85

Woolff, A. 'Apartheid and economics in Anglo-Saxon England' in Higham, NJ (ed.), *Britons in Anglo-Saxon England,* (2007): 115–129

Yorke, B. 'Early Anglo-Saxon Kingdoms', reported in: *Battle & District Historical Society Journal,* Vol. 14, 2009

Yorke, B. *Kings and Kingdoms of early Anglo-Saxon England,* (1990)

Yorke, B. *Nunneries and the Anglo-Saxon Royal Houses,* (2003)

Web Bibliography

This listing is up to date at the time of publication. As noted in the text such sources can change, be re-sited, or disappear and UK web publishers are urged to lodge their websites with the British Library Open UK Web Archive. If items have been moved or re-named, they may be findable via a web search engine. If they have been deleted and had a UK domain name it is suggested that the Open UK Web Archive is searched.

Alfred the Great, The Last Will and Testament of	http://blogs.bl.uk/digitisedmanuscripts/2013/07/the-last-will-and-testament-of-alfred-the-great.html
Anglo-Saxon Nuns and Nunneries in Southern England	https://www.reading.ac.uk/web/files/GCMS/RMS-1989-05_B._Yorke,_%27Sisters_Under_the_Skin%27_AngloSaxon_Nuns_and_Nunneries_in_Southern_England.pdf
ARCHI – collated lists of archaeological finds	https://www.archiuk.com/
Battle and District Historical Society Collectanea papers	http://battlehistory.btck.co.uk/Collectanea-OurVirtualLibrary/
Belgic England	www.ancestraljourneys.org/belgicengland.shtml
British Museum (Mountfield hoard)	https://www.britishmuseum.org/research/collection_online/collection_object_details.aspx?objectId=1394774&partId=1&technique=17235&sortBy=imageName&page=1
Digital Atlas of the Roman Empire	https://dh.gu.se/dare/
E-Sawyer an online updated version of Peter Sawyer's Anglo-Saxon Charters: an Annotated List and Bibliography (RHS, 1968)	https://esawyer.lib.cam.ac.uk/about/index.html
East Sussex Historic Environment Record (ESHER)	https://www.thekeep.info/east-sussex-historic-environment-record-her/

Flood maps	http://flood.firetree.net/ Please use with care as the maps do not take into account historical changes in the coastline, only sea level changes on present day geography
Hastings Area Archaeological Research Group	http://www.haarg.org.uk/home
Great Domesday for Sussex papers: Hull project	https://hydra.hull.ac.uk/resources?f%5Bsubject_topic_sim%5D%5B%5D=Great+Domesday&page=10 (accessed 3 June 2020)
Hastings Chronicle informative and updating history of Hastings and St Leonards	https://hastingschronicle.net/
Lyminge pre-Viking minster and its associated settlement	www.reading.ac.uk/web/files/archaeology/Lyminge_Research_design.pdf
Noticia Dignitarum - Militarium in partibus Occidentis.	1876 printed book in Latin https://archive.org/details/notitiadignitat00silvgoog/page/n5
Noticia Dignitarum - Militarium in partibus Occidentis.	Script book in Latin http://www.imperium-romana.org/notitia-dignitatum.html Note: In 'Noticia Dignitarum' See Sections VII. 100; XXVIII. 10, 12 & 20; XLI.17 and XLII.24
OpenDomesday	https://opendomesday.org/
PAS - Portable Antiquities Scheme	https://finds.org.uk/
PASE- Prosopography of Anglo-Saxon England	http://www.pase.ac.uk/
Sussex Coast, Past and Present	http://www.sussex.ac.uk/geography/researchprojects/coastview/Introduction_background/Sussex_blue_book_coasts.pdf
Sussex Archaeological Society	https://sussexpast.co.uk/

Sussex Place Names Net (Coates, R. (2007). Locus focus: forum of the Sussex Place-Names Net 1996-2007)	https://uwe-repository.worktribe.com/output/3497575/locus-focus-forum-of-the-sussex-place-names-net-1996-2007
Sussex Records Society	https://www.sussexrecordsociety.org/
UK Web Archive	https://www.webarchive.org.uk/ukwa/
Wareham - Anglo-Saxon church, Lady St Mary	http://www.anglo-saxon-churches.co.uk/marywareham.html
Wareham Priory	http://www.pastscape.org.uk/hob.aspx?hob_id=456709

Index